THE
ARIZONA
GUN OWNER'S
Guide

Who
can bear arms?

Where
are guns forbidden?

When
can you shoot to kill?

by Alan Korwin

illustrations by Gregg Myers

BLOOMFIELD PRESS
Phoenix, AZ

BLOOMFIELD PRESS

12629 N. Tatum #440T
Phoenix, AZ 85032
(602) 996-4020

ISBN 0-9621958-3-9

ATTENTION
Clubs, Organizations, Firearms Training Instructors,
Educators and all interested parties: Contact the publisher for
information on quantity discounts!

Every gun owner needs this book—
it doesn't make sense to own a gun and not know the rules.

Printed and bound in the United States of America

20 19 18 17 16 15 14 13 12

TABLE OF CONTENTS

ACKNOWLEDGMENTS

This book is really the result of all the help I received, great and small, from the good people who shared their thoughts and resources with me. Thank you.

Landis Aden, Legislative Liaison,
 Arizona State Rifle and Pistol Association
Terry Allison, President,
 Arizona State Rifle and Pistol Association
Ben Avery, *Arizona Republic* columnist,
 Co-author of Arizona's gun laws
Mark Barnett, Community Relations Officer, Scottsdale Police
Bob Cecil, Protection and Compliance Manager,
 Arizona State Land Department
Bob Corbin, Attorney General, State of Arizona
Nelson E. Ford, Owner, The Gunsmith, Inc.
Howard Gillmore, Assistant Director/Field Services,
 Parks and Recreation
Lt. Colonel Michael Haran, Staff Judge Advocate,
 Arizona Army National Guard
Wayne J. Higgins, Criminal Investigator,
 Bureau of Indian Affairs, Phoenix
Don Jansen, Director, Arizona Legislative Council
Mark Jecker, Public Information Officer,
 Arizona Game and Fish Department
Wes Keys, Information Coordinator,
 Arizona Game and Fish Department
Tony Machukay, Executive Director,
 Arizona Commission on Indian Affairs
Marty Mandall, Owner, Mandall Shooting Supplies, Inc.
Jordan Meschkow, Registered Patent Attorney
Richard B. Oxford, Director, Contract and Records Division,
 Arizona State Land Department
Mary Peterson, NRA Representative
Ron Peterson, Inspector,
 Bureau of Alcohol, Tobacco and Firearms, Phoenix Branch
Ruth Peterson, Secretary to the Forest Supervisor,
U.S. Forestry Service
Bob Reyes, Park Operations Specialist, National Parks Service
Robert J. Spillman, Attorney at Law
Paul Stearns, Police Officer, Scottsdale Police Department
Deborah Stevens, Public Affairs Specialist,
 Bureau of Land Management

Russell Vanden Wolf, Inspector,
   Bureau of Alcohol, Tobacco and Firearms, Phoenix Branch
Ken Wagner, Chief of Operations Section, Arizona State Parks
Pete Weinel, Assistant Recreation/Wilderness Staff,
   U.S. Forest Service

This list would be incomplete without the friends who have been supportive, informative, and whose time and thoughts made a real difference: Harvey and Eileen Barish, Linda Brott, Steve Cascone, Crosby!, Candice DeBarr, Adam Mohney, Gregg Myers, Bill Plummer, Curt Prickett, Dan and Mary Sharayko, Pete Slater, Mary Westheimer and Howard White.

The National Rifle Association Institute allowed the use of material in their pamphlet, "Your State Firearms Laws."

For the first edition of this book, March 1989:
Illustrations by Gregg Myers
Book design by Ralph Richardson
Edited by Howard White
Proofread by Candice DeBarr
Typesetting by Mesa Graphics, Inc.
Digital disk transfers by Code Busters

For the re-plated eleventh edition of this book, June 1994:
Document scans and OCR by Directional Data, Inc.
Legislative and update assistance by Landis Aden,
John Gilbert, Gwen Henson, Jim Norton, Edward J. Owen,
Ted Parod and Richard Twitchell
Proofread by Toni Joyce
Typesetting, editing and updated design by the author

◆

The people who have contributed to this book since it first appeared five years ago are too numerous to mention. You know who you are. Thank you.

PREFACE

Arizona has strict gun laws. You have to obey the laws. There are serious penalties for breaking the rules.

Many gun owners don't know all the rules. Some have the wrong idea of what the rules are. It doesn't make sense to own a gun and not know the rules.

Here at last is a comprehensive book, in plain English, of the laws and regulations which control firearms in Arizona.

FOREWORD • WARNING! • DON'T MISS THIS!

This book is not a substitute for the law. You are fully accountable under the exact wording and current interpretations of all applicable laws and regulations when you deal with firearms under any circumstances.

Many people find laws hard to understand, and gathering all the relevant ones is a lot of work. This book helps you with these chores. Collected in one volume are the principal state laws controlling gun use in Arizona.

In addition, the laws and other regulations are expressed in regular conversational terms for your convenience. While great care has been taken to accomplish this with a high degree of accuracy, **no guarantee of accuracy is expressed or implied, and the explanatory sections of this book are not to be considered as legal advice or a restatement of law.** In explaining the general meanings of the laws, using plain English, differences inevitably arise, so **you must always check the actual laws.** The author and publisher expressly disclaim any liability whatsoever arising out of reliance on information contained in this book. New laws and regulations may be enacted at any time by the authorities. **The author and publisher make no representation that this book includes all requirements and prohibitions which may exist.**

This book concerns the gun laws as they apply to law-abiding private residents in the state of Arizona only. It is not intended to and does not describe most situations relating to licensed gun dealers, museums or educational institutions, local or federal military personnel, American Indians, foreign nationals, the police or other peace officers, any person summoned by a peace officer to help in the performance of official duties, persons with special licenses (including collectors), non-residents, persons with special authorizations or permits, bequests or intestate succession, persons under indictment, felons, prisoners, escapees, dangerous or repetitive offenders, criminal street gang members, delinquent, incorrigible or unsupervised juveniles, government employees, or any other people restricted or prohibited from firearm possession.

While this book discusses possible criminal consequences of improper gun use, it avoids most issues related to deliberate gun crimes. This means that certain laws are excluded, or not explained in the text. Some examples are: 1st degree murder; 2nd degree murder; homicide; manslaughter; concealment of stolen firearms; enhanced penalties for commission of crimes with firearms, including armed robbery, burglary, theft, kidnapping, drug offenses and assault; smuggling firearms into public aircraft; threatening flight attendants with firearms; possession of contraband; possession of a firearm in a prison by a prisoner; false application for a firearm; shooting at a building as part of a criminal street gang; removal of a body after a shooting; drive by shootings; and this is only a partial list.

The main relevant parts of Arizona state laws which relate to guns are reproduced in Appendix D. These are formally known as *Arizona Revised Statutes,* and are mostly found in *Title 13, Criminal Code.* Many other state laws which may apply in some cases, such as Hunting Laws and official agency regulations, are discussed but these laws are *not* reproduced. Key federal laws are discussed, but the laws themselves are *not* reproduced. Case law decisions, which effect the interpretation of the statutes, are *not* included.

FIREARMS LAWS ARE SUBJECT TO CHANGE WITHOUT NOTICE. You are strongly urged to consult with a qualified attorney and local authorities to determine the current status and applicability of the law to specific situations which you may encounter. A list of the proper authorities appears in Appendix C.

Guns are serious business and require the highest level of responsibility from you. **What the law says and what the authorities and courts do aren't always an exact match.** You must remember that each legal case is different and frequently lacks prior court precedents. A decision to prosecute a case and the charges brought may involve a degree of discretion from the authorities involved. Sometimes, there just isn't a plain, clear-cut answer you can rely upon. **ALWAYS ERR ON THE SIDE OF SAFETY.**

Special Note on Pending Legislation

Many new bills have been proposed by legislators who would:
- Outlaw specific or classes of firearms by name, by operating characteristics, or by appearance
- Restrict the amount of ammunition a gun can hold and the devices for feeding ammunition
- Restrict the number of firearms and the amount of ammunition a citizen may buy or own
- Require proficiency testing and periodic licensing
- Register firearms and owners nationally
- Use taxes to limit firearm and ammunition ownership
- Create new liabilities for firearm owners, manufacturers, dealers, parents and persons involved in firearms accidents
- Outlaw keeping firearms loaded or not locked away
- Censor classified ads for firearms and eliminate firearms publications
- Melt down firearms that are confiscated by police
- Prohibit gun shows
- Abolish hunting
- Repeal the Second Amendment to the Constitution

In contrast, less attention has been paid to laws that would:
- Mandate school-based safety training
- Provide general self-defense awareness and training
- Encourage personal responsibility in resisting crime
- Protect citizens who stand up and act against crime
- Fix the conditions which generate hard-core criminals
- Assure sentencing of serious criminals, increase the percentage of sentences which are actually served, provide more prison space and permanently remove habitual criminals from society
- Improve rehabilitation and reduce repeat offenses
- Reduce plea bargaining and parole abuses
- Close legal loopholes and reform criminal justice malpractice
- Reform the juvenile justice system
- Improve law enforcement quality and efficiency
- Establish and strengthen victims' rights and protection
- Apply the assets from firearm confiscations to increase law enforcement resources
- Provide for the common defense and buttress the Constitution

Some experts have noted that easy-to-enact but ineffectual "feel good" laws are being pursued instead of the much tougher course of laws and social changes which would reduce crime and its root causes. Many laws aim at disarming citizens while ignoring the fact that gun possession by criminals is already strictly illegal and largely unenforced. Increasing attacks on the Constitution and civil liberties are threatening freedoms Americans have always had. You are advised to become aware of any new laws which may be enacted. Contact your legislators to express your views on proposed legislation.

To my wife Cheryl,
my daughter Tyler,
my brother Richard,
and my parents.

THE RIGHT TO BEAR ARMS 1

In the United States of America, citizens have always had the right to bear arms. The Second Amendment to the United States Constitution is the foundation of this right to have and use guns. The Second Amendment is entitled The Right To Keep And Bear Arms. This is what it says:

> "A well regulated Militia, being necessary to the security of a free State, the right of the people to keep and bear Arms, shall not be infringed."

The intentions of the revolutionaries who drafted the Constitution were clear at the time. It was this right to bear arms which allowed those citizens 200 years ago to break away from British rule. An armed populace was a precondition for independence and freedom from oppressive government. The founders of the United States of America wanted it to stay that way:

"No free man shall be debarred the use of arms."
–Thomas Jefferson

"The Constitution shall never be construed to authorize Congress to prevent the people of the United States, who are peaceable citizens, from keeping their own arms."
–Samuel Adams

"Little more can reasonably be aimed at with respect to the people at large than to have them properly armed."
–Alexander Hamilton

"Americans have the right and advantage of being armed."
–James Madison

"The great object is that every man be armed. Everyone who is able may have a gun." **–Patrick Henry**

Today the issue is controversial and emotionally charged. There are powerful and vocal groups on all sides of the topic of guns. Some people have taken to saying that the Second Amendment doesn't mean what it always used to mean, and there have been calls to repeal it. The Supreme Court has been mostly quiet on the subject, and its few pronouncements have been used to support all sides of the debate. Importantly, all 50 states recognize a citizen's right to act in self-defense, completely apart from firearms debates.

Nothing in Arizona law may conflict with the U.S. Constitution, and so the right to bear arms is passed down to Arizonans, as it is to the citizens of all the states in the union. The states, however, have passed laws to organize and control the arms which people bear within their borders. That's what this book is about.

The majority of the Arizona "gun laws" are in a book called, *Arizona Revised Statutes, Title 13, Criminal Code.* It is widely available in libraries, and a complete official copy may be obtained from The Michie Company—see the details on the back page of this book. An excerpt of the main relevant sections of the state gun laws are printed in Appendix D. Many of the fine details concerning guns come from other sources, listed in Appendix C.

The "§" (section) symbol used in this book refers to the related section of the Arizona Revised Statutes, which can be found in Appendix D.

REASONS FOR ARIZONA'S GUN LAWS

Arizona criminal law begins with a list of reasons for its existence (§13-101), all of which have direct impact on gun ownership and use:

1–To prohibit conduct which might harm people;

2–To give fair warning of conduct which is against the law and the penalties involved;

3–To define the acts which are crimes and to limit condemnation of behavior which isn't criminal;

4–To organize crimes by how bad they are, and to match the penalty to the crime;

5–To discourage crime by authorizing punishment;

6–To mete out punishment;

7-To promote truth and accountability in sentencing.

WHAT IS A FIREARM?

In Arizona, a firearm is defined as a *deadly weapon,* a term which includes anything designed for lethal use. Specifically, §13-105 of state law says that "firearm" means:

> "...any loaded or unloaded pistol, revolver, rifle, shotgun or other weapon which will or is designed to or may readily be converted to expel a projectile by the action of expanding gases..."

An exception is made for a firearm which is permanently inoperable. This applies primarily to antique or collectible guns which have been thoroughly disabled and are only for show. Questions about how to make a specific gun unserviceable can be directed to the Firearms Technology Branch of the Bureau of Alcohol, Tobacco and Firearms.

All other antique, replica, curio, relic and similar firearms capable of firing (or which can be modified to fire) are treated as ordinary guns under state law.

A B•B, pellet or dart gun (using compressed air or CO_2 gas to propel the projectile) fits the main definition of a firearm.   B•B guns are sometimes treated as regular firearms by the authorities, and are specifically mentioned in a few regulations. However, when describing criminal misconduct with a firearm, §13-3101 of the law uses a special definition for guns, in which the projectile is expelled by "the action of an explosive."   This clearly excludes a B•B gun's operation, but when in doubt, the safest course of action is to treat B•B guns as if they are regular firearms.

In this book, the words *gun, firearm* and *arms* are used interchangeably, and include handguns such as pistols and revolvers, and long guns such as rifles and shotguns.

WHO CAN BEAR ARMS IN ARIZONA?

Adults

If you are a resident of Arizona you may have a gun unless:

1–You have been found to be dangerous to yourself or other people by a court of law;

2–You have been convicted of a felony involving violence or possession and use of a deadly weapon or dangerous instrument, and your civil rights have not been restored;

3–You are serving a term of imprisonment in any correctional or detention facility.

Arizona law calls these people *prohibited possessors.* Knowingly selling or transferring a deadly weapon or ammunition to a prohibited possessor is a class 6 felony. Having a deadly weapon or ammunition if you are a prohibited possessor is a class 4 felony. See §13-3102 for the letter of the law.

In addition, you may also be prohibited from firearm possession under federal laws designed to keep weapons out of the hands of criminals. These overriding restrictions are listed in Section 8 of the Firearm Transaction Record, form 4473, which must be completed when you buy a gun from a federally licensed dealer. Federal law prohibits gun purchase or possession by anyone who:

• Is charged with or has been convicted of a crime which carries more than a one-year sentence (except for state misdemeanors with up to a two-year sentence);

• Is a fugitive from justice;

• Unlawfully uses or is addicted to marijuana, a depressant, a stimulant or a narcotic drug;

• Is mentally defective;

• Is mentally incompetent;

• Is committed to a mental institution;

• Has been dishonorably discharged from the armed forces;

- Has renounced U.S. citizenship;
- Is an illegal alien

When filling out a Firearm Transaction Record form, you are required to state that you are not in any of these categories. It is a felony to make false statements on a Firearms Transaction Record form.

Keep in mind that the right to bear firearms isn't the right to bear anything, anywhere, at any time. Nor is it the right to organize a body of armed individuals.

Juveniles
In general, a minor can only have or use a firearm if accompanied by a parent, grandparent or guardian. Detailed exceptions are listed below and under Hunting Regulations in Chapter 4. Giving or selling a gun, ammunition, or a toy gun which can expel dangerous or explosive substances to a minor, without written consent from the minor's parent or legal guardian, is a class 6 felony. With consent from a parent or guardian, temporary transfer of firearms and ammunition to minors by instructors for courses, competition or training is allowed, as is temporary transfer by adults accompanying minors for hunting or target practice. See §13-3109 for the letter of the law.

POSSESSION OF FIREARMS BY MINORS

For this rule, people under 18 who are unemancipated are minors. Minors cannot knowingly carry or have a gun on themselves, have a gun within their immediate control, or have a gun in or on a means of transportation. This applies to any place open to the public, on any street or highway, and on private property not owned or leased by the minor, the minor's parent, grandparent or guardian. See §13-3111 for the letter of the law.

This restriction does not apply if the minor is accompanied by a parent, grandparent, guardian, or certified gun-safety or hunting-safety instructor acting with the consent of the minor's parent or guardian. It also does not apply to people 14 to 17 who are:

- Legally hunting, or
- Transporting an unloaded gun to legally hunt, or
- At a shooting event or marksmanship practice at an established shooting range or at other areas where shooting is not prohibited, or transporting an unloaded gun to such places between 5 a.m. and 10 p.m.

A peace officer must immediately seize a firearm found in violation of this law, and it must be held by the agency which seized it until the charges have been duly settled. If the minor is found guilty, the firearm is forfeited, but if the authorities can identify the lawful owner of the firearm, it must be returned to that person. A minor who violates this law is deemed a delinquent child and:

- May have their driver's license suspended or revoked at court discretion, until they are 18, or if they don't have a license, the court may prohibit issuing a driver's license until the person is 18 years old, and
- May be fined up to $250 for an unloaded gun, and up to $500 for a loaded gun.
- If the offense involves possession of a loaded or unloaded firearm in a motor vehicle, the fine is up to $500 and the court must revoke or suspend the person's driver's

license, or if the person doesn't have one, prohibit issuing one until the person is 18 years old. The court may allow driving privileges limited to between home, school and work, specified to match the person's schedule, if no other means of transportation is available.

If you knew, or reasonably should have known, that your minor child was violating the law and you made no effort to stop it, you can be held responsible for the fines or actual civil damages resulting from illegal use of the firearm.

This law is in addition to any other laws concerning the use or exhibition of a deadly weapon, and a minor guilty of breaking this law may also be prosecuted and convicted on other charges.

This law, §13-3111, unlike every other state gun law, does not apply to the whole state, but only to counties with populations in excess of 500,000 (currently only Maricopa and Pima counties). Because it may be adopted in other counties, cities or towns it would be prudent to follow it statewide. The legislature, in passing this law, expressed the intent that this take precedence over local rulings, in keeping with the preemption statute, §13-3108. This would apply to cities which, while this law was being debated, disregarded preemption and enacted conflicting rules requiring minors to have parental permission slips for carrying firearms. Some municipalities may enforce those conflicting ordinances.

A separate education statute (§15-841) says that possession, display or use of a firearm by a pupil is grounds for expulsion from school. In addition, a person found to be delinquent loses the right to possess a firearm (§13-904).

HOW DO YOU OBTAIN FIREARMS?

Guns and ammunition may be bought or sold between private residents of this state under the same conditions as any other private sale of merchandise, provided you comply with all other laws (you can't sell to prohibited possessors, or to minors without their parent's or guardian's permission, etc.). Sale and delivery of firearms by a private resident to a non-resident is prohibited by federal law. Such sales must take place through licensed dealers in the two people's states, described later under transport and shipping. As long as all other laws are complied with, a non-resident may temporarily borrow or rent a firearm for lawful sporting purposes from a dealer or a resident. You may own any number of firearms and any amount of ammunition.

If you are going to deal in guns (or for that matter, import, manufacture or ship firearms in interstate or foreign commerce), you need a license from the Bureau of Alcohol, Tobacco and Firearms. Federally licensed dealers of firearms and ammunition are spread across the state. Residents need no special license or permit to walk in and buy a regular firearm from a regular dealer. Firearms may be paid for in the same ways as any other retail merchandise. You may sell a gun you own to any dealer in the state.

To purchase a handgun and matching ammunition you must be at least 21 years old. Your request to purchase a handgun from a dealer, if you don't have a concealed-weapon permit, is made on a written form and reported to local authorities, who must conduct a criminal-history background check, required by the Brady Law. A waiting period of zero to eight days applies while the check is conducted (see chapter 4 for more on the Brady Law).

To purchase a rifle or shotgun and matching ammunition you must be at least 18 years old, and there is no Brady waiting period or background check (see chapter 4 for changes that will occur if the Brady national instant background check is established). Some ammunition may be used in either a handgun or a rifle. This type of ammo

can only be sold to a person between the ages of 18 and
21 if the dealer is satisfied that it will be used only in a rifle.

Arizona Handgun Clearance Center
Effective Oct. 1, 1994, the Department of Public Safety is
required to establish an instant background check system
for handgun purchasers in this state. Known as the Arizona
Handgun Clearance Center, once it is set up, it eliminates
the paperwork and waiting period of the Brady Law (which
the Brady Law allows for under paragraph s-1-D), and allows
dealers to check a person's credentials on the spot. If the
Brady Law is ever repealed, the Handgun Clearance Center
will also be repealed, automatically. See §13-3108.01 for
the letter of the law.

In-State Purchase
Personal ID that establishes your name, address, date of
birth and signature, and which has your photo if you want
to purchase a handgun, must be shown to the dealer. A
driver's license (or state ID card issued in place of a driver's
license) is the usual form of ID expected by most dealers.

When you buy firearms from a licensed dealer you must fill
out a federal Firearms Transaction Record, form 4473.
There are no duplicate copies made of this form, and the
original is permanently filed by the dealer. The form
requires personal identification information, identification
of the gun and its serial number, and your signature, stating
that you are not ineligible to obtain firearms under federal
law. Licensed dealers keep copies of this form available.

Additional requirements of the Brady Law are described in
chapter 4, but these are basically eliminated once the
Arizona Handgun Clearance Center is established, as
described above, on Oct. 1, 1994.

The purchase of more than one handgun from the same
dealer in a five-day period is reported to the Bureau of
Alcohol, Tobacco and Firearms and, under the Brady Law,
to local authorities as well, before the close of business on
the day of the sale.

Out-of-State Purchases

Residents of this state, including businesses and corporations, are specifically granted permission in the state statutes (§13-3106) to buy guns anywhere in the United States. Such purchases must conform to the local laws at the place of purchase. However, the overlapping local, state and federal gun laws in the U.S. are frequently incompatible, and can sometimes make this difficult.

When you buy a long gun out of state, you may take delivery immediately. Federal law requires that handguns purchased out of state must be shipped to you via a licensed dealer in your home state—you cannot take possession of the gun over the counter.

Gun Shows

Gun shows are periodically sponsored by national, state and local organizations devoted to the collection, competitive use or other sporting use of firearms. You may purchase firearms from an in-state dealer at a gun show the same as you could on their regular retail premises. Out-of-state dealers can display their wares and take orders, but cannot make deliveries at the show. Purchases made from an out-of-state dealer must be shipped to a licensee within this state, from the out-of-state dealer's licensed premises.

CARRYING FIREARMS

Open Carry

The following applies to adults who are not prohibited from firearms possession. You may carry firearms, loaded or unloaded, throughout the state of Arizona, subject to the restrictions which follow. If you carry a gun on yourself and you don't have a concealed-weapon permit, it must be at least partially visible or in a belt holster which is at least partially visible. See §13-3102 for the letter of the law.

You may also carry a gun in a scabbard or case designed for carrying weapons. The scabbard or case must be at least partially visible, or else carried in luggage.

The law is unclear concerning so-called fanny-pack holsters and feminine-protection handbags, designed for discreetly carrying firearms. While the law allows carry in a holster or case designed for carrying weapons as long as the holster or case is at least partially visible, it also prohibits concealed carry without a permit, which puts these increasingly popular devices in a gray area. The law does not define what a holster or case is or looks like.

Authorities and courts have been inconsistent in handling citizens who use these devices, from ignoring a person who has one to misdemeanor convictions, creating a substantial degree of risk. The risk is eliminated, however, if you have a concealed-weapon permit, which makes either device clearly acceptable.

Guns in Cars
You may carry a firearm, loaded or unloaded, anywhere in a car (or other means of transportation), in a case, holster, scabbard, pack or luggage, or if it is plainly visible. (See the special rules concerning guns in cars on school grounds.) A gun may also be out of sight in a storage compartment, trunk or the glove compartment of the vehicle, without violating the law. Without a concealed-weapon permit, it's illegal to have an unholstered gun otherwise concealed and within immediate control of any person in a car or other means of transportation. Violation is a class 1 misdemeanor. See §13-3102 for the letter of the law.

This rule causes a great deal of confusion because a gun may be concealed from sight in a car (in the glove box, for example) and still be legal, even without a permit. In a holster, a gun may be concealed anywhere in a car and not violate the law. The authorities, however, have been known to illegally ticket or arrest individuals, who are later found not guilty and released, especially for a holstered gun under the seat, making this popular carrying spot a risky choice. An *unholstered* gun under the seat, or under a hat or a newspaper is a good way to go to jail. No one ever said that these laws make a lot of sense, just that they are the laws.

CONCEALED WEAPONS

In Arizona, unless you have a concealed-weapon permit, it's generally against the law to carry a firearm (or any other deadly weapon) concealed on yourself. See §13-3102 for the letter of the law. Carrying a concealed weapon if you have no permit is a class 1 misdemeanor. Carrying concealed if you have a permit but don't have it with you is a class 2 misdemeanor. There are only three places where you may, without a permit, legally carry a concealed weapon on yourself in this state:

1–In your own dwelling;

2–On your business premises;

3–On real estate owned or leased by you.

Local, state and federal authorities may be permitted to carry concealed weapons. As of July 17, 1994, Arizona residents may also apply to obtain permits for carrying a concealed weapon.

Concealed-Weapon Permit

A permit to carry a concealed weapon (CCW) is available to any resident who is qualified as described below. See §13-3112 for the letter of the law. You must carry the permit with you whenever you carry a concealed weapon and must show it to any law enforcement officer on request. Failure to show the permit when asked is a class 2 misdemeanor.

The Department of Public Safety (DPS) maintains a computerized permit record system to confirm the validity of all CCW permits. If you are found without your permit while carrying a concealed weapon, DPS must be notified, and the permit will be immediately suspended. If your permit is suspended you must present it to the law enforcement agency that found you without it, or in a court. As soon as DPS is notified that you presented the permit, they will restore it.

If you are arrested or indicted for an offense that would disqualify you for a CCW permit after you have obtained one, the permit is immediately suspended and will be seized. If you are convicted of such an offense the permit will be revoked. If you are found not guilty, or if the charges are dropped or dismissed, you can have the permit restored by presenting documentation from the court or county attorney.

Possession of a valid Arizona concealed-weapon permit allows you to purchase a handgun from a licensed dealer without any delay or the additional background check and paperwork otherwise required by the Brady Law. The CCW permit satisfies the exclusion from Brady under paragraph s-1-C of that law.

CCW Application
DPS is required by law to issue your CCW permit if you:

1–Are an Arizona resident;

2–Are at least 21 years of age;

3–Are not under indictment for and have not been convicted of a felony in any jurisdiction;

4–Do not suffer from mental illness and have not been adjudicated mentally incompetent or committed to a mental institution;

5–Are not an illegal alien;

6–Pass a DPS-approved firearms safety training program. Honorably retired federal, state or local peace officers, with at least 10 years of service, do not have to take the training program.

To apply for a CCW permit you must complete a DPS Concealed Weapon Permit/Firearms Safety Training Instructor Approval Application Form A, available from either approved training organizations, most hunting and fishing license locations or directly from DPS. The form requires your name, address, social security number, driver's license number and state, home and business telephone, race/origin, sex, height, weight, eye and hair color, and date and place of birth.

There are check boxes to indicate if you are applying for a new permit, a renewal, or certification as a trainer, a set of boxes confirming that you are an eligible applicant (no prior felonies, etc., as listed above), and a place for your signature and the date. You are not required to identify the firearm you will carry, which means you can use your permit with any firearm you prefer when you carry. Filling out the form untruthfully is perjury, a class 4 felony. A complete CCW-permit application includes:

1–Concealed Weapon Permit Application form.

2–Certificate of successful completion of a DPS-approved training program (this appears on the back of the application form and is filled out by the trainer);

3–Two sets of fingerprints (the law stipulates two sets, DPS is currently asking for only a single set);

4–A fee set by the DPS Director, currently $50, which must be paid by cashier's check, certified check or money order, payable to Arizona Department of Public Safety. Cash and personal checks are not accepted. The fee is non-refundable.

You should also note that:

• If the form is incomplete or all the elements are not submitted the application will not be processed.

• Only original DPS forms are accepted—do not send photocopies, but you should keep a photocopy for your own records.

• A fingerprint card is provided with the application form, which you must take care of on your own—DPS will not take your prints. Local police departments, private firms (listed under Fingerprinting in the phone book) or your trainer can take care of this for you.

Application Background Checks
When DPS receives your completed application, they conduct a background check and may send your fingerprints to the FBI for a national check. DPS must by law complete all checks in 60 days, and if you pass, issue your permit within 15 working days of your qualifying. Although the forms indicate that you should allow 75 days for processing, department policy is to process applicants as quickly as practical. They do not accept calls inquiring about the status of an individual permit application.

Application Denials

If DPS denies your permit after the qualification check, they must notify you in writing within 15 working days and state why your application was denied. When you receive the denial, you have 20 days to submit additional documentation to DPS. When DPS receives this material they must reconsider their decision and, within 20 days, inform you of their reconsideration. If you are denied again, you have the right to appeal in Superior Court.

Duration

A permit is valid for up to four years and is renewable every four years. To renew you must complete a DPS-approved four-hour refresher course and pay a fee. Since the first renewals will not fall due until mid-1998, the refresher requirements and the amount of the fee may not be established for a while. DPS must conduct a background check within 60 days of receiving your renewal application, before your permit can be renewed. DPS will suspend or revoke your permit if you have become ineligible and will notify you in writing, stating the reasons, within 15 working days of the suspension or revocation.

MANDATORY CONCEALED-WEAPON TRAINING

The Department of Public Safety (DPS) is required, under the provisions of §13-3112, to establish minimum standards for concealed-weapon-training programs and instructors. Any resident who seeks a permit to carry a concealed weapon (CCW) must take and pass an approved course.

An organization seeking to provide CCW-permit training applies to DPS for approval on a Firearms Safety Training Program Approval Application Form B, which is included in the packet with the Concealed Weapon Permit Application Form A. Any organization "legitimately doing business in the state of Arizona," may apply. DPS must approve a program if:

1–The course is at least 16 hours in length;

2–It is conducted on a pass or fail basis;

3–It covers the following topics in a format approved by the DPS Director:

- Safe handling and storage of weapons,
- Weapon care and maintenance,
- Legal issues relating to the use of deadly force,
- Mental conditioning for the use of deadly force,
- Marksmanship,
- Judgmental shooting;

(Program details are described in a four-page outline which accompanies the application forms. These are covered below under Minimum Course Requirements.)

4–The instructors meet DPS-qualification standards and have passed a background investigation, including a check for warrants, a criminal history records check and submission of two sets of fingerprints which may be sent to the FBI. (The law stipulates two sets of prints, DPS is currently requiring only one set.);

5–The organization has paid a fee to DPS. (DPS is currently waiving the fee requirement for organizations, but the instructors themselves must pay a fee to be qualified.)

With the application, potential training organizations are required to include a detailed subject/topic outline of their proposed program, including a set of correctly answered test questions. DPS is required to safeguard the proprietary interests of all approved instructors and training programs, and cannot disclose the contents of a program except to proper authorities or by court order. An appeals process is available, described in §13-3112-Q, for organizations whose training program is not approved.

Minimum Course Requirements
DPS has established these minimum training requirements:

1–Familiarization with loading, unloading and accessories for single action and double action revolvers, and single, double and select action semiautomatic pistols.

2–Firearms choices for handling comfort, stopping power, controllability and holstering options.

3–Safety issues, including the basic safety rules, gun safes, locking devices, ammunition storage, loaded firearms in the home and training household members.

4–Legal information from A.R.S. Title 4 (liquor laws); Title 13 (criminal law) including chapters 4 (justification), 5 (responsibility), 12 (assault), 13 (kidnapping), 15 (trespass and burglary), 29 (public order), 31 (weapons and explosives); and federal, county and other states' laws as relevant.

5–Shooting techniques including isosceles stance, Weaver and modified-Weaver stances, one- and two-hand grip options, dominant eye, sight alignment, sight picture, target identification, trigger contact and trigger control (continuous pressure vs. continuous anticipation).

6–Judgmental shooting for shoot/don't shoot situations.

7–Behavior for contact with law enforcement officers while carrying a concealed weapon, declaring CCW, approaching law enforcement during volatile situations, responsibilities for reporting shooting incidents.

8–Mental conditioning for use of deadly force, including white, yellow, orange and red modes of awareness, critical-incident stress and post-shooting trauma.

9–Gun cleaning and maintenance, level of disassembly, unloading weapon, field stripping, cleaning procedures, lubrication and safety checks for re-assembly.

10–A written 10-question test, developed independently by each DPS-authorized training organization, that students must complete with a minimum score of 70% at the end of the class.

11–A ten-round marksmanship test, at an NRA TQ15 target or equivalent (where the secondary scoring ring is not greater than 14" x 16"), without time limit, 5 rounds fired at 5 yards and 5 rounds fired at ten yards, with shots outside the secondary scoring ring not counting as hits, that students complete with at least 70% accuracy.

It's worthwhile noting that some training organizations conduct classes which exceed the minimum requirements, providing an enhanced training opportunity.

Instructor Qualifications

The same application form used to apply for a permit is used to apply for approval as a CCW trainer. The fee for a trainer is $100, which includes a CCW permit, or $74 without the permit. Trainer applicants must submit clear copies of their qualifying certifications—do not send originals since they will not be returned. Approved trainers can only teach through organizations whose programs have been approved. To be eligible trainers must have at least one of the following certifications:

- ALEOAC (Arizona Law Enforcement Officer Advisory Council)/AzPOST (Arizona Police Officer Standards and Training Board) Arizona Basic Police Firearms Instructor Certification

- NRA Police Firearms Instructor Development School

- NRA Law Enforcement (Security) Firearms Instructor Development School

- NRA Personal Protection Instructor rating *and* NRA Pistol Instructor rating. (If you are in this category you may be required to receive some additional instruction or information. A new "special" Personal Protection course has been developed to cover areas required by the CCW law but which are not part of the standard

Personal Protection program. The new program requires you to demonstrate ability to safely handle a revolver and a semiautomatic handgun, qualify with both on the range, pass a basic handgun knowledge test at the beginning of the course, and pass a 100-question written test at the end of the program. These requirements are subject to change.)

A person with sufficient prior training or approval to conduct CCW training may be able to obtain a permit without further training. Check with DPS for applicability.

Notes:

DPS maintains records comparing the number of permits requested, issued and denied, and reports the information annually to the governor and the legislature.

A special hotline telephone number is available for any questions you may have about the concealed weapons program. In the Phoenix area call the DPS Handgun Clearance and Permit Section at 256-6280. Outside the Phoenix area call toll-free, 1-800-256-6280.

PROHIBITED PLACES

Many of the restrictions on possession of firearms are found in §13-3102 of the criminal code. Other prohibitions are found in federal, land office and agency regulations, codes and laws.

- You cannot enter any public establishment or attend any public event and carry a deadly weapon after the people in charge of the establishment or event make a reasonable request for you to give them custody of the weapon. Failure to place the weapon in their custody is a class 1 misdemeanor. A sign prohibiting weapons at an entrance point is considered a reasonable request.
- Going into a polling place with a gun, on the day of an election, is a class 1 misdemeanor.
- Bringing or having a gun in a commercial nuclear generating station is a class 1 misdemeanor.
- It's a class 1 misdemeanor to have a firearm on school grounds. Exceptions are described below.
- You can't have a gun in a federal facility, except while hunting or for other legal reason. You cannot be convicted of this violation unless notices are posted. See the details below.
- It's a class 2 felony to bring a gun into a correctional facility or its grounds.
- It's a class 5 felony to bring a gun into or around a juvenile correction facility.
- Except for limited hunting privileges, there is a fine of up to $500 for carrying a gun in the National Parks.
- Possession of firearms on a military base is subject to control by the commanding officer.
- Firearm possession is prohibited on the gate side of airport passenger security checkpoints.
- On a game refuge, possession of a loaded gun for taking game, without special written permission from the Arizona Game and Fish Commission, is a class 2 misdemeanor.

School Grounds

It's generally illegal to have a gun on school grounds. Knowingly having a firearm on school grounds is a class 1 misdemeanor, unless:

- It is directly related to hunter or firearm safety courses; or

- It is for use on the school grounds in a program approved by a school; or

- It is unloaded within a means of transportation under the control of an adult. If the adult leaves, the vehicle must be locked and the gun must not be visible from outside.

A school is a public or nonpublic kindergarten program, common school, or high school. A violation of this law is a class 1 misdemeanor unless it occurs in connection with other specified crimes, in which case it is a class 6 felony. See §13-3102 for the letter of the law. School personnel must immediately report violations to the school administrator, who must immediately report violations to a peace officer. See chapter 4 for federal regulations.

Federal Facilities

Guns are generally prohibited in federal facilities. Knowingly having a gun or other dangerous weapon (except a pocket knife with a blade under 2-1/2 inches) in a federal facility is punishable by a fine and up to one year imprisonment. Exceptions include authorities performing their duties, possession while hunting, or other lawful purpose. You cannot be convicted unless notice of the law is posted at each public entrance, or if you had actual notice of the law. A federal facility is a building (or part), federally leased or owned, where federal employees regularly work.

Bars

It is generally illegal to have a firearm in a place which is licensed to serve alcohol. If you walk in and don't know it's illegal you're excused once. (The law says it's illegal to walk in with a firearm "knowing such possession is prohibited"). Having a gun in a bar is a class 2 misdemeanor. See §4-244 for the letter of the law.

It's illegal for the licensee of a bar to allow a person with a firearm to remain on the premises. It's illegal for the licensee to supply you with liquor knowing you're armed. These are both class 2 misdemeanors. A licensee must call the police to remove an armed person, if necessary. The State Liquor Board can suspend, revoke, or refuse to renew a liquor license for failure to comply.

The law allows a few exceptions:

1–Hotel and motel guest accommodations are excluded.

2–The licensee of a bar, and employees who the licensee authorizes, may carry firearms.

3–A liquor-licensed establishment can have an exhibition or display of firearms in connection with a meeting, show, class or similar event.

4–If you enter a bar to seek emergency aid, and you receive no alcohol, you may legally carry firearms.

Transport and Shipping
You may ship and transport firearms around the country, but not by the U.S. Postal Service, under the oldest federal firearms statute on the books, dating from Feb. 8, 1927. You may have a weapon shipped to a licensed dealer, manufacturer or repair shop and back. However, depending upon the reason for the shipment and the shipper being used, the weapon may have to be shipped from and back to someone with a federal firearms license. You should check with the intended recipient and you must inform the shipping agent in writing before shipping firearms or ammunition.

Any purchased gun which is shipped interstate must go from a licensed dealer to a licensed dealer. Many dealers in the state will act as a "receiving station" for a weapon you purchase elsewhere, sometimes for a fee.

If you buy a gun from a private party out of state, the gun may only be shipped to a licensed dealer within Arizona. If you sell a gun to a private party out of state, the gun must be shipped via a licensed dealer in the purchaser's state.

The only time when you may directly receive an interstate shipment of a gun is the return of a gun which you sent for repairs, modification or replacement to a licensee in another state.

Personal possession of firearms in other states is subject to the laws of each state you are in. Federal law guarantees the right to transport a gun in a private vehicle, if you are entitled to have the gun in your home state and at your destination, if the gun is unloaded and locked in the trunk, or in a locked compartment other than the glove compartment or the console if the vehicle has no trunk.

Common or Contract Carriers

You may transport firearms and ammunition interstate by "common carriers" (scheduled and chartered airlines, buses, trains, ships, etc.), but you must notify them in writing and comply with their requirements. Call in advance and get precise details and the names of the people you speak with—you wouldn't be the first traveller to miss a departure because of unforseen technicalities and bureaucratic runarounds.

For air travel, firearms must be unloaded, cased in a way deemed appropriate by the airline, and may not be possessed by or accessible to you in the "sterile" area anywhere on the gate side of the passenger security checkpoint, including on the aircraft. Your firearms may be shipped as baggage, or you may give custody of them to the pilot, captain, conductor or operator for the duration of the trip. Airlines are required to comply with firearms rules found primarily in the Code of Federal Regulations, Title 14, Sections 107 and 108, and, along with other carriers, with the United States Code, Title 18, section 922. Under the Brady Law, carriers may not identify the outside of your baggage indicating that it contains a firearm, a prime cause for theft in the past.

Transit Risks

Traveling with personal firearms presents certain risks. The authorities have been known to hassle, detain or arrest people who are legally traveling with weapons, due to confusion, ignorance, personal bias and for other reasons, even when those reasons are strictly illegal. Some authorities have openly challenged or defied existing legal safeguards for law-abiding firearms owners. As a practical matter, because each state's laws differ and there is no easy way to determine what each state's laws are, the right to bear arms as you travel interstate may be seriously infringed.

Local Ordinances

Arizona's Criminal Code prohibits local authorities from passing firearms laws which conflict with state statutes. This is called preemption, and is found in §13-3108. Despite this rule, some cities have enacted laws which appear to conflict with state law. For example, in 1993 some cities required armed juveniles to have parental permission slips which state law doesn't recognize, and Tempe has issued a ban on firearms in a downtown area on weekends. A possession restriction was on the books in Tombstone for nearly a century, predating the preemption statute. It originated from the shoot-out at the OK Corral, and was repealed in 1994.

Most local firearm ordinances merely reiterate state statutes, giving city courts jurisdiction in some areas. This typically has no direct effect on law-abiding gun owners, but the new conflicting laws might. *It is important to note that* The Arizona Gun Owner's Guide *does not cover local ordinances, whether they agree or conflict with state law.* The liability to citizens who obey state laws that conflict with local laws is uncertain and creates a degree of risk.

WHAT DO YOU NEED TO GET A FIREARM?

- You must be over 18 years old for a long gun, over 21 for a handgun;
- You need an ID which establishes your name, address, date of birth and signature, and has a photo for a handgun purchase;
- If you don't have a concealed-weapon permit, you must file a form with the dealer and wait from zero to eight days to meet the Brady Law requirements (see Chapter 4) before taking delivery of a handgun (the wait and paperwork does not apply for a long gun). Once the Arizona Handgun Clearance Center "instant check" is established in October, 1994, the waiting and paperwork of the Brady Law are eliminated;
- If you have a CCW permit you are excluded from the Brady paperwork, background check and delay;
- If you are not an Arizona resident, it must be legal for you to have the weapon in your home state. You may take possession of a long gun over the counter, but if you are purchasing a handgun it must be shipped to a dealer in your home state—you cannot take possession of it here; and
- You must be able to pay for your purchase.

WHEN CAN YOU CONCEAL A FIREARM?

WHEN CAN YOU CONCEAL A FIREARM?

Unless you have a valid Arizona concealed-weapon permit, the question isn't *when,* it's *where.*   The three *places* where you may conceal a gun on yourself are:

1 – In your residence;

2 – On your business premises;

3 – On land owned or leased by you.

For private citizens without a permit, there are no other "times" allowed under the law.

Confusion occasionally arises since, in some cases, a gun may be concealed from sight without being a violation of the concealed weapons laws.   Two common examples would include a gun in a gun case (as long as the case is at least partially visible or carried in luggage) and a gun in a glove box, both of which are permissible without a permit.

With a valid concealed-weapon permit, you can carry concealed anywhere in the state, except for the prohibited places listed in this chapter.

WHAT DOES IT ALL MEAN?

Law books don't use the word *crime*—they use the terms *felony, misdemeanor* and *petty offense*. Crimes are divided into these categories to match the punishment to the crime. Felonies are extremely serious, misdemeanors are serious and petty offenses can be serious.

Felonies and misdemeanors are also grouped into "classes." *Class 1* means the worst crime. Felonies go from class 1 to class 6, and include fines and jail terms of six months or more. Misdemeanors run from class 1 to class 3, and include fines and jail terms of six months or less. Petty offenses have no class, and include fines only.

See the Crime and Punishment Chart on the inside back cover for the basic penalties for each type of crime.

TYPES OF WEAPONS 2

There are weapons and there are weapons. A gun may be perfectly legal, but if you put it in your pocket it becomes a *concealed weapon* and that's a crime unless you have a concealed-weapon permit. If a gun has been modified in certain ways, it becomes a *prohibited weapon* and it may be a crime to possess it at all.

Weapons include *dangerous instruments,* things which can be deadly depending on their use, like fireplace tools or a baseball bat. *Deadly weapons* specifically refers to things which are designed for lethal use. Guns are only one kind of deadly weapon, and CCW-permit holders may carry weapons other than guns.

Concealed-weapon-permit applicants are required to have an understanding of the different types of firearms, their methods of operation, selections for personal defense, holstering options, ammunition types, loading and unloading, cleaning and maintenance, accessories and more. Many fine books cover these areas, and any gun owner ought to be familiar with such information. This chapter of *The Arizona Gun Owner's Guide* only covers weapons from the standpoint of those which are illegal, restricted or otherwise specially regulated.

PROHIBITED WEAPONS

In 1934, responding to mob violence spawned by Prohibition, Congress passed the National Firearms Act (NFA), the second federal law concerning guns since the Constitution (a postal regulation was first). This was an attempt to control what Congress called "gangster-type weapons." Items like machine guns, silencers, short rifles and sawed-off shotguns were put under strict government control and registration. These became known as "NFA weapons."

This gave authorities an edge in the fight against crime. Criminals never registered their weapons, and now simple possession of an unregistered "gangster gun" was a federal offense. Failure to have paid the required transfer tax on the weapon compounded the charge. Regular types of personal firearms were completely unaffected.

Political assassinations in the 1960s led to a public outcry for greater gun controls. In 1968 the federal Gun Control Act was passed, which absorbed the provisions of earlier statutes, and added bombs and other destructive devices to the list of strictly controlled weapons. Arizona calls these *prohibited weapons,* though a more accurate title might be *controlled weapons,* as you'll see under Machine Guns. It is generally illegal to make, have, transport, sell or transfer any prohibited weapon without prior approval and registration. Violation of this is a class 4 felony under state law, and carries federal penalties of up to 10 years in jail and up to a $10,000 fine.

Defaced Deadly Weapons
Removing, altering or destroying the manufacturer's serial number on a gun is a class 6 felony. Knowingly having a defaced gun is a class 6 felony. See §13-3102 for the letter of the law.

Federal Weapon Bans
Congress has been considering a variety of selective and categorical firearms bans. Although none have been

enacted as this edition of *The Arizona Gun Owner's Guide* went to press, citizens would be well advised to follow developments and remain keenly aware of any firearms or accessories which were formerly legal and then declared illegal.

ILLEGAL GUNS
(Also called NFA weapons or prohibited weapons)

These weapons and destructive devices are among those that are legal only if they are pre-registered with the Bureau of Alcohol, Tobacco and Firearms.

1–A rifle with a barrel less than 16 inches long

2–A shotgun with a barrel less than 18 inches long

3–A modified rifle or shotgun less than 26 inches overall

4–Machine guns

5–Silencers of any kind

6–Firearms over .50 caliber

Guns with a bore of greater than one-half inch are technically known as destructive devices. Some antique and black powder firearms have such large bores but are not prohibited, as determined on a case-by-case basis by the Bureau of Alcohol, Tobacco and Firearms.

A number of other deadly weapons which are not guns are also prohibited under state and federal law:

OTHER ILLEGAL DEADLY WEAPONS
(Also called destructive devices)

Possession of these devices is a class 4 felony (§13-3102):

1–Explosive, incendiary or poison gas bombs

2–Explosive, incendiary or poison gas grenades

3–Explosive, incendiary or poison gas rockets with more than 4 ounces of propellant (includes bazooka)

4–Explosive, incendiary or poison gas mines

5–Mortars

6–Molotov cocktails

7–Nunchaku (a martial arts weapon made of two sticks, clubs, bars or rods, connected by a rope, cord, wire or chain. Nunchaku are not prohibited in lawful martial arts pursuits.)

8–Armor piercing ammunition (a handgun bullet with at least a core of steel, iron, brass, bronze, beryllium, copper, depleted uranium, or one or a combination of tungsten alloys. Excluded are nontoxic shotgun shot, frangible projectiles designed for target shooting, projectiles intended for industrial purposes, oil- and gas-well perforating devices, and ammunition which is intended for sporting purposes.)

9–Missiles with an explosive or incendiary charge greater than 1/4 ounce.

MACHINE GUNS

Under strictly regulated conditions, private citizens can have weapons which would otherwise be prohibited. An example is the machine gun.

Unlike normal firearm possession, the cloak of privacy afforded gun ownership is removed in the case of so-called "NFA weapons"—those which were originally restricted by the National Firearms Act of 1934. The list has grown since that time, through subsequent legislation. For a law-abiding private citizen to have an NFA weapon, five conditions must be met. These requirements are designed to keep the weapons out of criminal hands, or to prosecute criminals for possession.

1–The weapon itself must be registered in the National Firearms Registry and Transfer Records of the Treasury Department. This list of arms includes about 193,000 machine guns.

2–Permission to transfer the weapon must be obtained in advance, by filing "ATF Form 4 (5320.4)" available from the Bureau of Alcohol, Tobacco and Firearms.

3–An FBI check of your background is performed to locate any criminal record which would disqualify you from possessing the weapon. This is done with the help of a recent 2" x 2" photograph of yourself and your fingerprints on an FBI form FD-258 Fingerprint Card, which must be submitted with the application.

4–The transfer of the weapon from its lawful owner to you must be federally registered. In other words, a central record is kept of every NFA weapon and its current owner.

5–You must pay a $200 transfer tax. For some NFA weapons, the transfer tax is $5.00.

A properly licensed dealer can sell a registered machine gun to a qualified private buyer.

You may apply for approval to make NFA weapons, such as short rifles or sawed-off shotguns. The application process is similar to the process for buying such weapons. Unregistered NFA weapons are contraband, and are subject to seizure. Having the unassembled parts needed to make an NFA weapon counts as having one.

The authorities are generally exempt from these provisions. Open trade in automatic weapons in Arizona is allowed between manufacturers and dealers, and includes state and city police, prisons, the state and federal military, museums, educational institutions, and people with special licenses and permits.

The official trade in machine guns is specifically prohibited from becoming a source of commercial supply. Only those machine guns (and other NFA weapons) which were in the National Firearms Registry and Transfer Records as of May 19, 1986 may be privately held. This includes about 6,600 machine guns in Arizona. The number available nationally will likely drop, since no new full-autos are being added to the registry, and the existing supply will decrease through attrition. Arizona has about 18,000 NFA weapons in total.

CURIOS, RELICS AND ANTIQUES

Curios and relics are guns which have special value as antiquities, for historical purposes, or other reasons which make it unlikely that they will be used currently as weapons. The Curio and Relic List is a 60-page document available from the Bureau of Alcohol, Tobacco and Firearms. They can also tell you how to apply to obtain curio or relic status for a particular weapon.

Antique firearms, defined as firearms with matchlock, flintlock, percussion cap or similar ignition systems, manufactured in or before 1898, and replicas meeting specific guidelines, are exempt from certain federal laws. For complete details contact the Bureau of Alcohol, Tobacco and Firearms. Remember, though, that if it can fire or readily be made to fire it is a firearm under state law.

NOTES

WHAT'S WRONG WITH THIS PICTURE?

These weapons and destructive devices are illegal unless they are pre-registered with the Bureau of Alcohol, Tobacco and Firearms.

- A rifle with a barrel less than 16 inches long
- A shotgun with a barrel less than 18 inches long
- A modified rifle or shotgun less than 26 inches overall
- Machine guns or machine pistols
- Silencers of any kind
- Firearms using fixed ammunition over .50 caliber
- Armor-piercing ammunition
- Explosive, incendiary or poison gas bombs
- Explosive, incendiary or poison gas grenades
- Explosive, incendiary or poison gas mines
- Explosive, incendiary or poison gas rockets with more than 4 ounces of propellant (includes bazooka)
- Missiles with an explosive or incendiary charge greater than 1/4 ounce
- Mortars

Keep in mind that additional weapons may be added to this list in the future.

WHERE CAN YOU SHOOT? 3

Once you own a gun, it's natural to want to go out and fire it. If you've decided to keep a gun, you should learn how it works and be able to handle it with confidence. Public ranges provide an excellent and safe opportunity. Many people also enjoy shooting outdoors on open terrain.

The 72.5 million acres of Arizona are regulated by many different authorities. The Bureau of Land Management (BLM) has a map available called the *Surface Management Responsibility* map, which gives an excellent overview of what's what. The map has certain limitations, not the least of which is its issue date, 1979, but it is a valuable reference nonetheless. Exact up-to-date records are kept by BLM, and an updated map is expected out in the future.

In order to understand where you can shoot outdoors in this state, you must first know where you cannot shoot. The restrictions come first when determining if shooting in an area is permissible.

Certain legal justifications may allow shooting, even if it would otherwise be illegal. An example is self-defense. A list of justifications is in Chapter 4.

GENERAL RESTRICTIONS

Illegal Trajectory
It is illegal to shoot if the bullet will travel anywhere where it may create a hazard to life or property. In National Forests, you may not shoot from or across a body of water adjacent to a road.

Aside from being a violation of several laws, there is a general rule of gun safety here: Be sure of your backstop. Take this a step further: Be sure of your line of fire. Never fire if you are unaware of (or not in full control of) the complete possible trajectory of the bullet. Be sure that the shot poses no threat to life or property.

The Quarter-Mile Rule
Shooting while hunting is prohibited within one-quarter mile of any residence or building that could serve as a residence whether occupied or not, or any other developed facility of any kind. Another vehicle (other than your own) counts as an object which you must be at least a quarter of a mile away from when you discharge your firearm.

Although this rule comes from and applies specifically to hunting regulations, authorities use the quarter-mile rule as a guideline for determining if gun use is safe. Don't take chances. Make sure you are *at least* a quarter of a mile from *anything* when you are shooting.

From Vehicles
It's illegal to fire a gun (without a handicap permit) from a vehicle while hunting. This includes an automobile, pickup, off-road vehicle, motorcycle, aircraft, train, powerboat, sailboat, floating object towed by a sailboat or powerboat or any device designed to carry a person. (Requirements for hunting waterfowl are different.) It's also illegal to knowingly shoot upon, from, across or into a road or railway while hunting, or while in the National Forests.

Once again, hunting regulations provide restrictions which aren't specifically regulated in most other state statutes. However, authorities frown on "road shooting," and it is extremely unsafe. Shooting from vehicles or on or around roads is not a good idea.

Posted Areas
Signs can be posted which restrict firearm use, possession, or access to land or premises.

- *Private Land* may be posted by authority of the landowner or lessee.

- *State Land* may be posted by the lessee, but only with permission from the Commissioner of the Arizona State Land Department.

- *National Forests* may have areas posted for a number of reasons by the authorities.

- *The Arizona Game and Fish Department* can post an area to restrict hunting.

Even *a store,* or any other *public place* or *public event* can post a sign restricting firearm possession. Most private, local, tribal, state and federal authorities may legally post an area under their control. The penalty for a violation varies depending upon who posted what area.

THE LAND OF ARIZONA

Bureau of Land Management Land (BLM)
16% of the state's land—about 12 million acres—is managed by BLM under a doctrine of multiple use and sustained yield. What this means is that recreationists share the lands with ranchers, miners and other users. BLM land is as close as there is to truly "public land."

The Arizona state BLM office in Phoenix maintains the maps (called Master Title Plats) and the current records on land status for the entire state. It is an invaluable resource for determining what land is what. Two maps published by BLM are excellent general references for shooters. The *Surface Management Map* provides an overview of the whole state at a glance. The *Wilderness Status Map* shows all BLM areas under special restrictions as wilderness preserves.

Shooting on BLM land is legal as long as you comply with the normal state regulations. A few special considerations apply:

- Observe posted closures. BLM land generally isn't posted, although main entry points may have signs. Special Management Areas and other sections may have posted restrictions.
- Avoid conflicts with lessees.
- Avoid developed areas.
- The Long Term Visitor Area (LTVA) of La Posa in the Yuma district, and the land within one-half mile of the LTVA is closed to shooting and hunting.
- It's illegal to willfully deface, disturb or destroy any personal property, natural object or area, structures, or scientific, cultural, archaeological or historical resource.
- It's illegal to willfully deface or destroy plants or their parts, soil, rocks or minerals.

Hunting on BLM land is allowed, subject to the regulations of the Arizona Game and Fish Department. However, BLM authorities can close sections to shooting, or restrict or close access to public lands, when and where safety or other valid reasons may require.

Knowingly and willfully violating BLM regulations carries a maximum $1000 fine and up to one year in jail. Violators may be subject to civil damages as well. BLM district offices are listed in Appendix C.

Cities

It is usually illegal to shoot within the boundaries of any city in the state. Municipalities are a no-fire zone, and can have their own special regulations prohibiting shooting within city limits. State law makes this a class 2 misdemeanor. The exceptions are described below.

- *Firing Ranges*—Shooting within city limits can be allowed on a properly supervised range. See "Shooting Ranges" in this chapter for a description of such ranges.

- *B•B Guns*—Individual cities may have their own rules concerning B•B guns. It may be permissible to set up a B•B gun range indoors or outdoors within municipal boundaries if proper safety measures are taken. Check with local authorities for exact details on your location.

- *Designated Hunting Ranges*—An area within a city may be designated a hunting area by the Arizona Game and Fish Department. If the chief of police of the city agrees and posts proper notices, then shooting is legal. This allowance can be revoked anytime the authorities decide it is unsafe.

- *Control of Nuisance Wildlife*—A required permit is available for this purpose from the Arizona Game and Fish Department or from the United States Fish and Wildlife Service. Problems with nuisance wildlife can often be handled best by contacting an exterminator who has the proper permits.

- *Special Permit*—The chief of police of a city may issue a special permit for firing guns within city limits.

- *Legally Justified Instances*—The law allows shooting within city limits under certain narrow circumstances called *justification*. An example is self-defense. For details see Chapter 4.

County Land

The state of Arizona is divided into 15 counties: Apache, Cochise, Coconino, Gila, Graham, Greenlee, Lapaz, Maricopa, Mohave, Navajo, Pima, Pinal, Santa Cruz, Yavapai and Yuma. In nine of these, the only lands generally owned by the county are small parcels which contain the sheriff's office, the county courthouse, the jail, vehicle depots or similar facilities.

In addition to administrative sites, six counties maintain a park system. The offices for the park systems of Coconino, Maricopa, Mohave, Navajo, Pima and Yavapai counties are listed in Appendix C.

County parks used to be open to firearm use, but because of increasing population and the relatively small sizes of these parks, firearm use is now extremely limited. In general, rifled firearms and target practice are prohibited in county parks. Shotgun (smooth bore) hunting on these lands is regulated by the Arizona Game and Fish Department. If and when prudent wildlife management requires, strictly controlled rifled firearm hunting may be allowed by AGFD in cooperation with the park authorities.

County land may contain authorized shooting ranges, and in fact one of the state's best equipped ranges, the Black Canyon Range, is on land leased by the Maricopa county parks.

Indian Country

Fourteen Indian tribes—better than 200,000 people—live in Arizona on 20 reservations. More than 19 million acres are included in this land, amounting to 28% of the state.

Each reservation maintains its own government, and operates almost as a separate nation. A Tribal Council, headed by a Chairman, Chairperson, President or Governor, makes laws regarding guns on Indian land. You must contact a specific reservation to get current information and valid permits for their land. No state license, permit or tags are required by the state for hunting in Indian Country. The address and telephone number for each reservation is listed in Appendix C.

Many reservations encourage hunting (and other use) of their land, with proper tribal permits and within regulations. Hunting does not necessarily mean firearms are allowed. For example, hunting is permitted by the Navajos on the largest reservation in the state, but a tribal code prohibits the use of firearms. Some tribes offer no guidelines on the subject.

Overlapping federal, state, tribal and local authority creates confusion when laws are violated in Indian Country. Enforcement of laws on Indian reservations can cause a fundamental conflict over jurisdiction. Actual penalties for violations may be the subject of dispute. The Arizona Commission on Indian Affairs calls for the federal government to take ultimate responsibility for prosecution of crimes committed on Indian lands by non-Indians.

National Forests

15% of Arizona—about 11 million acres—is made up of National Forests operated by the Forest Service of the U.S. Department of Agriculture. You may carry firearms at anytime and anywhere in the National Forests, as long as you and your gun are in compliance with the law. Don't confuse the National Forests with the National Parks (listed later), where you normally may not even carry a loaded gun.

Hunting is allowed in the National Forests, but requires proper licenses. Contact the Arizona Game and Fish Department for details. Also see the separate section on "Hunting Regulations" in Chapter 4.

Target shooters are required to use removable targets. Clay pigeons, bottles, trash and other targets which leave debris are prohibited. Your choice of a target site should be against an embankment which will prevent bullets from causing a hazard. Your location should be remote from populated sites.

The laws controlling the National Forests are in a book called *Code of Federal Regulations, Title 36,* available at larger libraries. These federal rules prohibit shooting:

- Within 150 yards of a residence, building, campsite, developed recreation site or occupied area;
- Across or on a Forest Development road;
- Across or on a body of water adjacent to a Forest Development road;
- In any way which puts people at risk of injury or puts property at risk of damage;
- Which kills or injures any timber, tree or forest product;

- Which makes unreasonable noise;
- Which damages any natural feature or property of the United States.

Violation of these restrictions carries a possible $500 fine and a maximum prison sentence of 6 months under federal law.

The Forest Supervisor or other proper authority may issue special restrictions on firearm possession or use, or close a section to access if it seems necessary to protect public safety, or for other good reason.

For example, a small section of Tonto National Forest known as the "Lower Salt River Recreation Area" has been closed to guns and B•B guns, *except* for licensed hunting, since October 1985, for safety reasons. The Superstition Wilderness within Tonto National Forest has had a similar restriction in effect since February 1985. In the Sabino Canyon Recreation Area you may not even *have* firearms, except for hunters passing through to the hunt area. It's always wise to check with a representative of the Forest Service about any piece of National Forest land you're planning on using. National Forests and their offices in the state of Arizona are listed in Appendix C.

National Parks Service Land
The National Parks Service of the U.S. Department of the Interior manages 22 national sites in Arizona, more than any other state. This includes National Parks, National Monuments, National Historic Sites and National Recreation Areas.

Limited hunting privileges exist in National Recreation Areas by special agreement of the Department of the Interior and the Arizona Game and Fish Department. Except for this, it's illegal to even carry a loaded firearm into the National Parks Service lands. Firearms must be unloaded, cased and out of sight, and broken down (bolt or magazine removed or otherwise temporarily inoperable). A list of Arizona's National Parks Service sites is in Appendix C.

Private Land

You can shoot on your own land as long as you don't violate any regulations. That means you need enough land to shoot safely, at least a quarter-mile from any roads, outside of municipal boundaries, without disturbing the peace, and so forth. 18% of Arizona—approximately 13 million acres—is owned privately or by corporations.

Land owners may grant permission for others to shoot on their land and may allow access to the public. Permission can be withdrawn at will. To prohibit shooting on private land, the landowner or lessee must put up plainly legible signs, at least eight by eleven inches in size, no more than a quarter-mile apart, around the entire protected area.

Shooting Ranges

Officially approved shooting ranges may be the best place to learn and practice the shooting sports. Ranges may be legally set up within city limits as long as they are operated by:

- A club affiliated with the National Rifle Association, The Amateur Trapshooting Association, The National Skeet Association, or any other nationally recognized shooting organization;
- Any agency of the federal government;
- An agency of state, county or city government which will have the range within its boundaries;
- Public or private schools.

For underground ranges on private or public property, only adult supervision is required. B•B guns may be used on a range operated with adult supervision.

State and Federal Military Land

Land reserved for military use, whether under the jurisdiction of the National Guard or a branch of the federal armed forces such as the Army or the Air Force, is controlled by a military commander. What a commander says, goes. Possession or use of firearms on a military base is subject to control by the commanding officer.

You can't do much of anything on military land without prior approval. In general, military shooting ranges are not available for public use. Where limited hunting privileges are available, they are subject to the regulations of the Arizona Game and Fish Department *and* the base commander. Anyone on military land is subject to a search. For details concerning a specific military installation, contact the base provost marshal or the base commander's office.

Carrying firearms while traveling on a public road which passes through military land is subject to standard state regulations.

State Land
13% of Arizona is managed by the Arizona State Land Department, and leased out under guidelines which require productive use of the land. You must have a permit to be on the nearly 10 million acres of state land. Trespassing is a class 2 misdemeanor.

State land, even though it may be under lease for grazing, agriculture, or any other purpose, is usually open to licensed hunting and fishing. Wildlife on state land belongs to the state, and so it is regulated by the Arizona Game and Fish Department.

A person with valid licenses and tags, engaging in a lawful hunt, is allowed on state land. In effect, a hunting license is a written exemption from the "No Trespassing - State Land" signs. Other people using the land, or hunters engaging in any other activities besides those normally involved in a lawful hunt, would be trespassing unless they had received special authorization.

Recreation permits are available for camping and other non-consumptive use of state land, but use of firearms is not included in these specially issued permits.

While you are on state land, it's illegal to intentionally or wantonly destroy, deface, injure, remove or disturb anything made and put there by people, or to harm or take away any natural feature, object of natural beauty, antiquity or other public or private property. A violation is a class 2 misdemeanor.

State Parks

Arizona has 25 state parks on about 45,000 acres of land. These are managed by Arizona State Parks. Hunting in the state parks is regulated by the Arizona Game and Fish Department.

Because of the relatively small size of these parks and the large number of people using them, use of firearms except for licensed hunting is discouraged. Shooting is illegal in and around developed areas of any kind. Firearms may be carried in the parks, but in park buildings or developed recreation areas, Park Rangers may request that you remove your weapons. Upon a reasonable request, you must either place the weapon in the Ranger's custody or leave the building or area.

WHAT'S WRONG WITH THIS PICTURE?

1–Shooting within city limits is normally prohibited.

2–It's illegal to shoot or harm a cactus.

3–It's illegal to deface signs.

4–Trespassing is illegal.

5–You can't use targets which leave debris.

6–Shooting at wildlife requires a permit or license.

7–The target has no backstop. The shooter is not controlling the entire trajectory of the bullet.

8–The shooter isn't wearing eye or ear protection.

THERE'S NOTHING WRONG WITH THIS PICTURE!

Practicing the shooting sports outdoors is all right as long as you comply with the laws.

- The shooters are at a remote location, on land which isn't restricted.
- The target leaves no debris.
- The target has a backstop which prevents bullets from causing a potential hazard.
- No wildlife or protected plants are in the line of fire.
- The shooters are using eye and ear protection.

WHERE ARE GUNS FORBIDDEN?

- You cannot enter any public establishment or attend any public event and carry a deadly weapon after the people in charge of the establishment or event make a reasonable request for you to give them custody of the weapon. Failure to place the weapon in their custody is a class 1 misdemeanor. A sign prohibiting weapons at an entrance point is considered a reasonable request.

- You can't bring a gun into a polling place on the day of an election.

- You can't carry a gun (except for licensed hunting) in the National Parks.

- You can't carry weapons on a military base without permission from the commanding officer.

- You can't have a loaded gun for taking game on a game refuge without written permission from the Arizona Game and Fish Commission.

- You can't bring a gun onto or around the grounds of a juvenile correctional facility, or in a prison or its grounds.

- You can't bring a gun into a place licensed to serve alcohol except for:
    - The boss, who can also authorize employees
    - Hotel or motel accommodations
    - Gun shows and similar events
    - For aid in an emergency, if you get no alcohol.

- You can't have a gun in a federal facility, except while hunting or for other legal reason. You cannot be convicted of this violation unless notices are posted.

- You can't have a firearm on school grounds except for hunter or firearm safety courses, or for an authorized school program. Exceptions for vehicles and transporting pupils are covered in chapters 1 and 4.

- Guns are forbidden in commercial nuclear generating stations.

- Gun possession is forbidden on the gate side of airport security checkpoints, the so-called "sterile" zone.

DEADLY FORCE AND RELATED LAWS 4

"I got my questionnaire baby,
You know I'm headed off for war,
Well now I'm gonna kill somebody,
Don't have to break no kind of law."

–from a traditional blues song

There are times when you may shoot and kill another person and be guilty of no crime under Arizona law. The law calls this *justification,* and says justification is a complete defense against any criminal or civil charges. See §13-401 and §13-413 for the letter of the law. The specific circumstances of a shooting determine whether the shooting is justified, and if not, which crime has been committed. Justification in killing someone does not provide criminal or civil protection for recklessly killing an innocent third person in the process. A stray shot you make can be as dangerous to you legally as committing a homicide.

Whenever a shooting occurs, a crime has been committed. Either the shooting is legal as a defense against a crime or attempted crime, or else the shooting is not justified, in which case the shooting itself is the crime.

USE OF DEADLY PHYSICAL FORCE

A reasonable person hopes it will never be necessary to raise a weapon in self-defense. It's smart to always avoid such confrontations. In the unlikely event that you must resort to force to defend yourself, **you are generally required to use as little force as necessary to control a situation. Deadly force can only be used in the most narrowly defined circumstances, and it is highly unlikely that you will ever encounter such circumstances in your life.** You have probably never been near such an event in your life so far. Your own life is permanently changed if you ever kill another human being, intentionally or otherwise.

No matter how well you understand the law, or how justified you may feel you are in a shooting incident, your fate will probably be determined much later, in a court of law. Establishing all the facts precisely is basically an impossible task and adds to your legal risks.

What were the exact circumstances during the moments of greatest stress, as best you remember them? Were there witnesses, who are they, what will they remember and what will they say to the authorities—each time they're asked—and in a courtroom? What was your relationship to the deceased person? How did you feel at the moment you fired? Did you have any options besides dropping the hammer? Can you look at it differently after the fact? Has there been even one case recently affecting how the law is now interpreted? Was a new law put into place yesterday? How good is your lawyer? How tough is the prosecutor? How convincing are you? Are the police on your side? Does the judge like your face? What will the jury think?

Be smart and never shoot at anyone if there is any way at all to avoid it. Avoiding the use of deadly force is usually a much safer course of action, at least from a legal point of view. You could be on much safer ground if you use a gun to protect yourself *without* actually firing a shot. Even though it's highly unlikely you'll ever need to draw a gun in self-defense, the number of crimes which are prevented by the presence of a citizen's gun—*which isn't fired*—are estimated to be in the millions. And yet, just pulling a gun can subject you to serious penalties. Think of it in reverse— if someone pulled a gun on you, would you want to press charges because they put your life in danger? You must be careful about opening yourself up to such charges.

Still, the law recognizes your right to protect yourself, your loved ones and other people from certain severe criminal acts. In the most extreme incident you may decide it is immediately necessary to use lethal force to survive and deal with the repercussions later. **You are urged to read the actual language of the law about this critical subject,** and even then, to avoid using deadly force if at all possible. Get the annotated criminal statutes in a library and read some case law to get a deeper understanding of the ramifications of using deadly force—and dealing with the legal system after the fact.

The Arizona Gun Owner's Guide **is intended to help you on a long journey to competence. Do not rely solely on the information in this book or on any other single source, and recognize that by deciding to prepare to use deadly physical force if it ever becomes necessary you are accepting substantial degrees of risk.**

Even with a good understanding of the rules, there may be more to it than meets the eye. As an example, shooting a criminal who is fleeing a crime is very different than shooting a criminal who's committing a crime. You may be justified in shooting to kill in a circumstance, and you might miss and only wound, but you can never shoot to intentionally wound. The law is strict, complex and not something to take chances with in the heat of the moment if you don't have to.

It's natural to want to know, beforehand, just when it's OK to shoot to kill and be able to claim self-defense later. Unfortunately, you will never know for sure until *after* a situation arises. You make your moves whatever they are, and the authorities or a jury decides. The law doesn't physically control what you can or can't do—it gives the authorities guidelines on how to evaluate what you did after it occurs. **There are extreme legal risks when you choose to use force of any kind.**

Because cases of murder outnumber cases of justifiable homicide, the authorities have a distinct tendency to think of the person holding a smoking gun as the perpetrator, and later as the defendant, while the person who gets shot, or was merely threatened with a gun, is the victim and in need of protection. If you ever come close to pulling the trigger, remember that there is a likelihood you will face charges when it's all over. The effects of the shot last long after the ringing in your ears stops.

The "§" (section) symbol used in this book refers to the related section of the Arizona Revised Statutes, which can be found in Appendix D.

"The quotations which follow are plain, conversational expressions of the gist of the law." This is followed by a more precise description of the law. Finally, each subject is cross-referenced to the actual section ("§") of the law.

Maintaining Order
"The person in charge can keep the peace."
If you are responsible for keeping order in a place where people are gathered you are justified in using deadly physical force if it is reasonably necessary to prevent death or serious physical injury. A person responsible for keeping order on a common motor carrier of passengers also has this justification. See §13-403 for the letter of the law.

Self-Defense
"Only when someone is about to kill you can you kill them first."
You are justified in threatening or using deadly physical force against another person to protect your life, only if a reasonable person would believe that your life is immediately and illegally threatened by the other person. If your life is being threatened by someone because of criminal activities you are doing, self-defense is probably not a valid claim. See §13-404 and §13-405 for the letter of the law.

The law says that if you provoke another person to attempt to use deadly force on you, you may lose your justification.

However, it also says that if you provoke someone, then back down and they don't back down, you may be justified. You are never justified in response to verbal provocation alone. See §13-404 for the letter of the law.

Defense of a Third Person
"You can protect someone else the same as you can protect yourself."
You are justified in threatening or using deadly physical force to protect a third person under the same circumstances as you would to protect yourself: if a reasonable person would believe that your actions are immediately necessary to protect the third person against the use of unlawful deadly physical force. See §13-406 for the letter of the law.

Defense of Premises
"You can't kill to protect your property, but you can threaten to protect it."
You or someone acting for you is justified in threatening to use deadly physical force in order to stop someone from criminally trespassing on your land or premises. Using deadly physical force is *not* justified unless you are actually defending your life, the life of a third person, or if one of the crimes listed under "Crime Prevention" (see below) is being committed. See §13-407 for the letter of the law.

Law Enforcement
"You can shoot to control certain criminal activities related to arrest and escape."
NOTE: On September 15, 1989, this section of the law was changed to prohibit a private citizen from shooting at a fleeing suspect. The language used to make the change unexpectedly altered other parts of this law, which basically describes your rights and limits for firearms use in law enforcement situations. For example, the new law now conflicts with the self-defense laws. Under certain circumstances it says if you are being shot at, you can only threaten to shoot back. Although some experts agree that this is an unintentional error needing correction, other experts feel it is acceptable as is. It is the law until changed

by the state legislature, and its effects on an actual case are uncertain. See §13-410 for the letter of the law.

Crime Prevention
"You can shoot to prevent certain crimes."
You are justified in using deadly physical force if you reasonably believe it is immediately necessary to prevent someone from committing:

1–Arson of an occupied structure (§13-1704); 2–First or second degree burglary (§13-1507, 8); 3–Kidnapping (§13-1304); 4–Manslaughter (§13-1103); 5–First or second degree murder (§13-1104, 5); 6–Sexual conduct with a minor (§13-1405); 7–Sexual assault (§13-1406); 8–Child molestation (§13-1410); 9–Armed robbery (§13-1904); 10–Aggravated assault (§13-1204, A, 1 & 2).

The law says you have no duty to retreat before threatening to use or using deadly physical force under the circumstances listed above, and that you are presumed to be acting reasonably if you are acting to prevent the commission of the crimes listed. See §13-411 for the letter of the law. However, several Arizona court cases have suggested that this law may only apply to situations involving your own home.

The idea that your home is your castle, the so-called "castle doctrine," does suggest that your justification in defending yourself at home is more secure than your justification out in public. In addition, if you have an obvious opportunity to retreat, especially if you're not at home, and you don't take it, your legal defense may be more difficult.

Domestic Violence
If a person has been a victim of domestic violence, their state of mind may be taken into account in certain justifiable homicides. See §13-415 for the letter of the law. A person who uses or threateningly displays a firearm during domestic violence (§13-3601) is subject to arrest.

RELATED LAWS

Use of firearms can lead to charges being brought against you if your actions are not justified by law. The basic penalties listed below may be significantly increased depending upon the circumstances.

Aggravated Assault
"You can't shoot or threaten to shoot someone without a legal reason."
Intentionally, knowingly or recklessly shooting a person (or causing serious bodily injury in any other way, for that matter) without legal justification, is aggravated assault, a class 3 felony. Threatening to shoot someone is also aggravated assault. See §13-1204 for the letter of the law.

Endangerment
"You can't just point a gun at someone."
It's against the law to recklessly put another person at substantial risk of imminent death or physical injury. When a risk of death is involved, endangerment is a class 6 felony. In all other cases, endangerment is a class 1 misdemeanor. See §13-1201 for the letter of the law.

Threatening or Intimidating
"You can't threaten a person with a gun."
Attempting to terrify anyone by threatening or intimidating them with physical injury or serious damage to their property is a class 1 misdemeanor. See §13-1202 for the letter of the law.

Disorderly Conduct
"You must act seriously with guns."
It's illegal to recklessly handle, display or fire a gun with the intention of or knowingly disturbing the peace and quiet of a neighborhood, family or person. This is a class 6 felony. Making unreasonable noise with the intention of or knowingly disturbing the peace and quiet of a neighborhood, family or person is a class 1 misdemeanor. See §13-2904 for the letter of the law.

Hindering Prosecution

<u>"It's illegal to help someone evade the law."</u>
Providing a person with a gun to help them avoid a felony, is a class 5 felony. Providing a gun to someone to help them avoid a misdemeanor or petty offense, is a class 1 misdemeanor. See §13-2510 thru 2512 for the letter of the law.

Criminal Nuisance

<u>"It's illegal to endanger other people."</u>
Recklessly creating or maintaining a condition which endangers the safety or health of others is a class 3 misdemeanor. See §13-2908 for the letter of the law.

Reporting Gunshot Wounds

<u>"It's a crime to treat a gunshot wound and not report it."</u>
A physician, surgeon, nurse or hospital attendant who is called on to treat a gunshot wound which may have resulted from illegal activity must immediately notify the authorities, and report the circumstances. Failure to make a report is a class 3 misdemeanor. See §13-3806 for the letter of the law.

Surrender of Weapons

<u>"A public place or event can request custody of your guns."</u>
You are required to surrender any deadly weapons in your possession if you are at a public establishment or event, and you are asked to do so by the people in charge. Failure to give custody of your weapons to the people in charge is a class 1 misdemeanor. See §13-3102 for the letter of the law.

Peace officers, members of the military, or other persons specifically licensed or authorized, in the performance of official duties, may be excluded from surrendering their weapons.

Forfeiture of Weapons

<u>"The authorities can take your weapons if they have just cause."</u>
Firearms may be seized by a peace officer during an arrest or search, or if the officer has probable cause to believe

that a firearm is subject to seizure. See §13-4305 for the letter of the law. If you have, use or display a firearm in violation of any public school rule, the firearm must be forfeited. See §13-2911 for the letter of the law. A firearm in the possession of a minor, unless it meets certain narrow exceptions, is subject to seizure. See §13-3111 for the letter of the law.

If you are convicted of a felony involving one or more guns, you forfeit the weapons. The state either keeps, sells or destroys them, as ordered by the court. See §13-3105 for the letter of the law.

Anyone making a lawful arrest may take weapons from the person arrested, and must turn the weapons over to the courts. See §13-3895 for the letter of the law.

Certain weapons are contraband if unregistered and are subject to seizure by the authorities. Included are weapons identified under the National Firearms Act as amended, or identified as prohibited weapons under state law.

Personal property, including firearms and ammunition, may be seized by the Bureau of Alcohol, Tobacco and Firearms when used or intended to be used or involved in violation of any U.S. laws which ATF agents are empowered to enforce. Acquittal or dismissal of charges allows you to regain any confiscated property.

Forfeiture of Rights
"Your right to bear arms can be lost."
Conviction of any felony removes your civil right to bear firearms under §13-904 and federal law. Also under §13-904 a minor found to be delinquent loses the right to bear arms. The right to bear arms is forbidden to anyone who is or becomes a prohibited possessor under federal law, as described in chapter 1 of this book, or as defined under §13-3102 of state law.

Responsibility
"Not everyone is equally criminally responsible for their acts."
A person under the age of fourteen when an offense occurs cannot be charged criminally for a shooting, unless

there is clear proof that the person knew the conduct was wrong when it took place (§13-501). A person who is guilty except insane at the time of commission of a criminal act is subject to special sentencing (§13-502). Temporary voluntary intoxication is not insanity and provides no defense for criminal acts (§13-503).

HUNTING REGULATIONS

Hunting regulations are complex, highly detailed and mandatory requirements issued annually by the Arizona Game and Fish Department (AGFD). The regulations are based on *Arizona Revised Statutes, Title 17*. You *must* get in touch with AGFD before even considering hunting or shooting at any wildlife. *The Arizona Gun Owner's Guide* only covers those parts of hunting rules which apply to firearms use.

The Arizona Game and Fish Department offers a 20-hour course of instruction which teaches safe handling of firearms, ethics and responsibilities, wildlife management and identification, survival, first aid and more. The course includes class and field work, and is open to anyone who is 10 years of age or older.

Land open to hunt is not always open to all shooting. Two small parts of Tonto National Forest, for example, are closed to all shooting except licensed hunting. Some land which may be hunted, like the 14-million-plus acres of the Navajo Indian Reservation for example, has a prohibition against firearms altogether.

Here are the key rules about using guns while hunting. Remember that hunting regulations are not limited to guns, and include bow and arrow and other devices.

• The Arizona Game and Fish Department specifies the types of guns and ammunition which are allowed when hunting each different type of game. The specifications are designed to help insure a quick clean kill. Different types of game may only be hunted in specified areas during specified seasons. It is illegal to otherwise hunt. Main hunting areas are on land regulated by the U.S.

Forest Service, the Bureau of Land Management, the State Land Department, Indian Country and private land.

- No one under ten years of age may hunt big game.
- No one between ten and fourteen years of age may hunt big game without having passed the Arizona Hunter Education Course offered by AGFD.
- A person between the ages of ten and fourteen may hunt wildlife other than big game without a license, if accompanied by a properly licensed hunter who is 18 years or older. There is a limit of two children per license holder.
- Anyone over 14 years of age needs a license to hunt wildlife.
- When hunting, you must have in your possession either a Class G General Hunting License, a Class F Combination Hunting and Fishing license, or a Class H Three-Day Hunting License (not valid for big game), plus any required tags, permit tags, or stamps.
- It's illegal to shoot while taking wildlife within a quarter mile of an occupied or possibly occupied farmhouse, cabin, lodge, trailer home or other building, without the permission of the owner or resident.
- It's illegal to shoot from a vehicle while hunting, without a special handicap permit. Special rules apply to hunting waterfowl.
- It's illegal to shoot from, across or into a road or railroad while hunting.
- It's illegal to be intoxicated while hunting.
- It's illegal to handle or fire a gun in a careless or reckless manner while hunting, or with wanton disregard for the safety of human life or property.
- A person involved in a shooting accident while hunting must:

    1–Render every possible assistance to the injured person;

    2–Immediately report the accident to and cooperate with the nearest law enforcement officer;

3–File a written report of the incident within 10 days to the Arizona Game and Fish Department.

- Poaching (hunting outside of the established regulations) is illegal and strongly discouraged. To anonymously report a suspected violation, call Operation Game Thief, 1-800-352-0700, 24 hours a day.

Rewards are anonymously paid for tips leading to arrests through the Operation Game Thief program, by AGFD and these organizations: Arizona Bowhunters Association, Tucson Rod and Gun Club, Arizona Desert Bighorn Sheep Society, Arizona Bowhunters and Field Archers Association, *Western Bowhunter* Magazine, Arizona Muzzleloading Association, Western Bowhunters Association, Central Arizona Bowhunters, Sportsman's Voice, Phoenix Varmint Callers and the Arizona Trapper's Association. Rewards can be as high as $1,000.

- It's illegal to have a gun for taking game within a game refuge, without special written consent of the Arizona Game and Fish Commission.

- Legal shooting time while hunting is during daylight hours. Weather conditions can alter actual times—you must be able to see well enough to shoot safely, to be legal. A few special exceptions apply.

- It's illegal to destroy, injure or molest livestock, growing crops, personal property, notices or signboards, or other improvements while hunting.

- It's illegal to shoot an animal and let any edible meat go to waste. Abandoning a carcass is illegal.

- Tracer ammunition, armor-piercing or full-jacketed bullets designed for military use are not allowed.

- Machine guns and silencers are not allowed.

- Semi-automatic centerfire rifles with a magazine capacity of more than five rounds are not allowed.

- Poisoned or explosive projectiles are not allowed.

- Shotguns larger than 10-gauge, or shotguns capable of holding more than two shells in the magazine are not allowed. Larger capacity shotguns must be plugged to limit the magazine to 2 shells.

- The use or possession of lead shot is prohibited in areas designated as nontoxic shot zones.
- Hunting with rifled firearms is prohibited within the Maricopa County Parks System. Limited deer hunting with rifled firearms, by special permit, may be allowed for a limited time by the Maricopa County Park Commission in cooperation with the Arizona Game and Fish Commission.
- Rifled firearms are prohibited in the Base and Meridian Wildlife Areas, and centerfire rifled firearms are prohibited in the Robbins Butte Wildlife Area. Many other Wildlife Area restrictions apply.
- A person participating in "archery-only" season may not use or possess a firearm.
- A person participating in "handguns, archery, and muzzle-loader (HAM)" season may not use or possess a long gun except a muzzle-loader.
- A special permit is available from the Phoenix office of AGFD which allows a physically disabled person to shoot from a motor vehicle, if a) the vehicle has a current handicapped license plate or disabled shooter's permit, b) is standing still, c) is not on a maintained public roadway, d) has its engine off, and e) is not used at any time to hunt or pursue wildlife.

Hunting Penalties
- Hunting license privileges may be revoked for up to five years for careless use of firearms resulting in human injury or death; destroying, molesting or injuring livestock; destroying or damaging crops, personal property, signs or other improvements; littering; letting someone else use your big game tag; or unlawful taking or possession of wildlife.
- Unless a penalty is otherwise specifically described by law, violation of hunting regulations is a class 2 misdemeanor.
- Taking wildlife, or attempting to obtain a hunting license while your hunting privilege is suspended is a class 1 misdemeanor.

- Knowingly taking, having or transporting big game unlawfully is a class 1 misdemeanor.
- Knowingly selling, bartering or offering for sale any big game which was taken unlawfully is a class 6 felony.
- Any peace officer who knowingly fails to enforce a hunting regulation is guilty of a class 2 misdemeanor.
- Anyone who unlawfully wounds, kills or has possession of certain wildlife is subject to civil suit by the Arizona Game and Fish Department in addition to other penalties. The list includes any endangered species, elk, bighorn sheep, buffalo, all eagles, deer, antelope, mountain lion, bear, turkey, javelina, beaver, goose, raptors, duck, small game animals, small game birds, game fish and non-game birds.

NOTES ON FEDERAL LAW

Dealers of firearms must be licensed by the Bureau of Alcohol, Tobacco and Firearms (ATF). Federal law requires licensed dealers to keep records of each sale. This information is permanently saved by the dealer but is otherwise uncollected. Paperwork required by the Brady Law is collected but must be destroyed shortly after it is used to conduct background checks, and no records of the checks may be kept.

This means there's no central place for anyone to go and see if a given individual owns a firearm. For someone to find out if you have a gun they would have to check all the records of all the dealers in the country, a daunting task. Only ATF is authorized to check the records of manufacture, importation and sale of firearms.

The dealer's records allow guns to be *traced,* a very different and important matter. When a gun is involved in a crime, ATF can find out, from the manufacturer's serial number, which licensed dealer originally received the gun. The dealer can then look through the records and see who purchased the weapon. It's a one-way street—a gun can be linked to a purchaser but owners can't be traced to their guns. One study of successful traces showed that four out of five were of some value to law enforcement authorities.

When President Reagan was shot by John Hinckley Jr., the weapon was traced and in fourteen minutes time, a retail sale to Hinckley was confirmed.

Buying, selling, having, making, transferring and transporting guns is in many cases regulated by federal laws. These regulations are covered in *The Arizona Gun Owner's Guide,* but for the most part, only state penalties are noted. There may be federal penalties as well.

Under the Assimilative Crimes Act, state law controls if there is no federal law covering a situation. Murder is a typical example of this. It is important to recognize that there can be a question of jurisdiction in some cases.

A long history of federal regulation exists with regard to firearms and other weapons. The main laws include:

- Second Amendment to the Constitution (1789)
- National Firearms Act (1934)
- Federal Firearms Act (1938)
- Omnibus Crime Control and Safe Streets Act (1968)
- Gun Control Act (1968)
- Organized Crime Control Act (1970)
- Omnibus Crime Control Act (1986)
- Firearm Owner's Protection Act (1986)
- Brady Handgun Violence Prevention Act (1993)

Additional federal requirements may be found in the Code of Federal Regulations and the United States Code.

Gun-Free School Zones Act

Federal law makes it illegal to knowingly have a firearm at a place which you know, or should reasonably believe, is a school zone. A school zone means in or on the grounds of an elementary or secondary public, private or parochial school, and the area within 1,000 feet from the grounds of the school. This does not apply to a firearm possessed:

- On private property not part of school grounds, or
- By a person duly licensed to possess firearms, if the license required the state's law enforcement authorities to verify that the person is qualified under law to receive the license (Arizona has no such license), or
- Which is unloaded and in a locked container, or a locked firearms rack which is on a motor vehicle, or
- By a person for use in a program approved by a school in a school zone, or
- By a person in accordance with a contract between a school in the school zone and the person or the person's employer, or
- Which is unloaded and possessed while traversing school premises to gain access to public or private lands open to hunting, if the entry on school premises is authorized by school authorities.

In addition, it's illegal to knowingly or with reckless disregard for another person's safety, fire or attempt to fire a gun at a place that you know is a school zone. This does not apply to firing a gun:

- On private property not part of school grounds, or
- By a person participating in a program approved by a school in the school zone, or
- By a person in accordance with a contract between a school in the school zone and the person or the person's employer.

Willful violation of this act carries a maximum fine of $5,000 and a maximum prison sentence of five years.

The Brady Law

The Brady Handgun Violence Prevention Act was signed into law on Nov. 30, 1993. Its provisions for common carriers, reporting multiple handgun sales and license fee increases are among the rules affecting private citizens which took effect immediately. The waiting-period provisions took effect on Feb. 28, 1994, and were set to expire on Feb. 27, 1999.

In addition to the regulation of private citizens described below, the Brady Law: places special requirements on dealers, sets timetables and budgets for the U.S. Attorney General to implement the law, provides funding, sets basic computer system requirements, mandates criminal-history record sharing among authorities, enhances penalties for gun thieves and more. Your federal legislators can send you the full 12-page Brady Law.

The Brady Law refers to a "chief law enforcement officer," defined as the chief of police, the sheriff, an equivalent officer or their designee. The description below refers to such persons as "the authorities." Where the law refers to an individual who is unlicensed under §923 of USC Title 18, this description says "private citizen" or "you." Federally licensed dealers, manufacturers and importers are referred to as "dealers." The act of selling, delivering or transferring is called "transferring." The law defines *handgun* as, "a firearm which has a short stock and is designed to be held and fired by the use of a single hand." A combination of parts which can be assembled into a handgun counts as a handgun.

Under the Brady Law, to legally obtain a handgun from a dealer you must provide:

- A valid picture ID for the dealer to examine;
- A written statement with only the date the statement was made, notice of your intent to obtain a handgun from the dealer, your name, address, date of birth, the type of ID you used and a statement that you are not: 1–under indictment and haven't been convicted of a crime which carries a prison term of more than one year, 2–a fugitive from justice, 3–an unlawful user of or addicted to any controlled substance, 4–an adjudicated

mental defective, 5–a person who has been committed to a mental institution, 6–an illegal alien, 7–dishonorably discharged from the armed forces, 8–a person who has renounced U.S. citizenship.

Then, before transferring the handgun to you, the dealer must:

• Within one day, provide notice of the content and send a copy of the statement to the authorities where you live;

• Keep a copy of your statement and evidence that it was sent to the authorities;

• Wait five days during which state offices are open, from the day the dealer gave the authorities notice, and during that time,

• Receive no information from the authorities that your possession of the handgun would violate federal, state or local laws.

The waiting period ends early if the authorities notify the dealer early that you're eligible. The authorities "shall make a reasonable effort" to check your background in local, state and federal records. Long guns are unaffected by the Brady Law until the National Instant Check described below comes on line.

You are excluded from the waiting-period process:
1–If you have a written statement from the authorities, valid for 10 days, that you need a handgun because of a threat to your life or a member of your household's life; 2–With a handgun permit, in the state which issued it, if the permit is less than five years old and required a background check (Arizona's concealed weapon permit qualifies, eliminating the need for permit holders to wait for handgun purchases or go through additional paperwork or background checks); 3–In states which have a handgun background check (Arizona's Handgun Clearance Center qualifies, required by state law to be established by Oct. 1, 1994, to conduct instant background checks for handgun purchasers, eliminating the need for residents to wait for handgun purchases or go through additional paperwork); 4–If the transfer is already regulated by the National Firearms Act of 1934, as with Class III weapons; 5–If the dealer has been

certified as being in an extremely remote location of a sparsely populated state and there are no telecommunications near the dealer's business premises.

If a dealer is notified after a transfer that your possession of the handgun is illegal, the dealer must, within one business day, provide any information they have about you to the authorities at the dealer's place of business and at your residence. The information a dealer receives may only be communicated to you, the authorities or by court order. If you are denied a handgun, you may ask the authorities why, and they are required to provide the reason in writing within 20 business days of your request.

Unless the authorities determine that the handgun transfer to you would be illegal, they must, within 20 days of the date of your statement, destroy all records of the process. The authorities are expressly forbidden to convey or use the information in your statement for anything other than what's needed to carry out the Brady process.

The authorities may not be held liable for damages for either allowing an illegal handgun transfer or preventing a legal one. If you are denied a firearm unjustly, you may sue the political entity responsible and get the information corrected or have the transfer approved, and you may collect reasonable attorney's fees.

National Instant Check: The Brady Law requires the U.S. Attorney General (AG) to establish a National Instant Criminal Background Check system (NICBC) before Nov. 30, 1998. Once this in effect, the previous waiting process is eliminated. In order to transfer any firearm, not just handguns, when the NICBC system is in place, a dealer must:

- verify your identity from a valid photo-ID card, contact the system, identify you and receive a unique transfer number, or
- wait three days during which state offices are open and the system provides no notice that the transfer would violate relevant laws.

The NICBC system is required to issue the transfer number if the transfer would violate no relevant laws, and it destroys all records of approved inquiries except for the identifying number and the date it was issued. If the transfer is legal, the dealer includes the transfer number in the record of the transaction. The NICBC system is bypassed under conditions similar to 2, 4 and 5 listed above as exceptions to the waiting period (with number 2 broadened to include "firearms" permit).

Whoever violates these requirements is subject to a fine of up to $1,000 and a jail term of up to 1 year.

If you are denied a firearm under the NICBC, you may request the reason and the system must present you with a written answer within five business days. You may also request the reason from the AG, who must respond immediately. You may provide information to fix any errors in the system, and the AG must immediately consider the information, investigate further, correct any erroneous federal records and notify any federal or state agency that was the source of the errors.

Multiple sales of handguns, (more than two from the same dealer in a five day period) are already reported to the Bureau of Alcohol, Tobacco and Firearms, and must now be reported to local authorities as well. Local authorities may not disclose the information, must destroy the records within 20 days from receipt if the transfer is not illegal and must certify every six months to the AG that they are complying with these provisions.

Common or contract carriers (airlines, buses, trains, etc.) may not label your luggage or packages to indicate that they contain firearms. (Federal law requires you to notify the carrier in writing if you are transporting firearms or ammunition. The long-time labeling practice had been responsible for the frequent theft of luggage containing firearms.)

Licensing fees for obtaining a new federal firearms license are increased to $200 for three years. The fee for renewing a currently valid license is $90 for three years.

Brady Law Note: While the Brady Law is new it would be prudent to anticipate a degree of confusion, inconsistent policies and enforcement, conflicting regulations and jurisdictions, regulations which do not match the letter of the law, denials of responsibility, and court cases to clarify the intent, practicalities and legality of the law. With the law being challenged in federal courts, changes to it, repeal or partial repeal are possible. The Bureau of Alcohol, Tobacco and Firearms is responsible for drafting the regulations to carry out the Brady Law and they may exercise a degree of discretion.

With the passage of Arizona's concealed weapon law in April, 1994, effective July 17, 1994, and the establishment of the state's instant check system in October of the same year, the waiting period and paperwork of the Brady Law are, well, eliminated entirely in Arizona.

Be aware that many new firearms laws have been proposed, some of which are listed in the front of this book. **New laws may be passed at any time, and it is your responsibility to be up to date when handling firearms under all circumstances.** Failure to comply with new laws and regulations can have serious consequences to you personally, even if you believe your Constitutional rights have been compromised, and in fact many experts have noted that increasing latitudes are being taken by some governmental authorities with respect to Constitutional guarantees. Legislative and regulatory changes present serious risks to currently law-abiding citizens, since what is legal today may not be tomorrow. The entire body of U.S. law is growing at a significant rate and it represents some potential for threats to freedoms Americans have always enjoyed. It is prudent to take whatever steps you feel are reasonable to minimize any risks.

IF YOU SHOOT A CROOK OUTSIDE YOUR HOUSE
DO YOU HAVE TO DRAG HIM INSIDE?

IF YOU SHOOT A CROOK OUTSIDE YOUR HOUSE DO YOU HAVE TO DRAG HIM INSIDE?

No! Acting on this wide-spread myth is a completely terrible idea. You're talking about tampering with evidence, obstructing justice, interfering with official procedures and more. If you're involved in a shooting, leave everything at the scene just as it is and call for the police and an ambulance.

Don't think for a minute that modern forensics won't detect an altered scene of a crime. At any shooting a crime has been committed. Either the shooting is justified, which means you were in your rights and the victim was acting illegally, or you exceeded your rights in the shooting, regardless of the victim's circumstance. The situation will be investigated to determine the facts, and believe it, the facts will come out. Police tell time-worn jokes about finding "black heel marks on the linoleum." And once you're caught in a lie, your credibility is shot.

If you tamper with the evidence, you have to lie to all the authorities to back it up. Then you have to commit perjury to follow through. Can you pull it off?

If the guy with the mask was shot from the front, armed as he is, the homeowner has a good case for self-defense. If the masked man was shot from behind, the homeowner has a case for acting to prevent 1st degree burglary. Either way, he's better off leaving the body where it falls.

Suppose you shoot an armed intruder coming through your window, and the body falls outside the house. You'll have a better time convincing a jury that you were scared to death, than trying to explain how the dead crook in your living room got blood stains on your lawn.

The reason this fable gets so much play is because there is a big difference between a homeowner shooting a crook in the kitchen, and one person shooting another outdoors. Shooting at a stranger outside your house can be murder.

CAN YOU POINT A GUN AT SOMEONE?

No matter how many aces a person is holding, you can't settle the matter with a gun. This also shows how the law can be interpreted in more than one way.

If the gun you draw is loaded, you create a substantial risk of imminent death, a class 6 felony called *endangerment*. (Without the risk of death endangerment is a class 1 misdemeanor.) Using a gun to put a person in reasonable fear of imminent physical injury is *aggravated assault*—a class 3 felony. A more lenient view would be to say that this is "reckless display of a gun," which is *disorderly conduct*, a class 6 felony. Merely flashing a gun can be *threatening or intimidating*, a class 1 misdemeanor. At the very least this is *criminal nuisance*, a class 3 misdemeanor.

When you go to court, it could be argued that this is actually *attempted murder*, a class 2 felony. And if the guy with the gun is angry enough to take back his money, it becomes *armed robbery*, also a class 2 felony.

By drawing your gun, the other guy may be able to shoot you dead and legally claim self-defense. You may never pull a gun to leverage an argument.

If someone pointed a gun at you, would you get angry and want to see them arrested? Consider how someone would feel if your roles were reversed, and it was you who pulled the gun when it wasn't absolutely necessary to prevent a life-threatening situation.

Despite all this, the law recognizes your right to defend yourself, your loved ones, and other people. The law also recognizes a citizen's right to act to prevent certain crimes. These cases, when you *can* point a gun at another person, are described in Chapter 4.

HOW CAN YOU CARRY A GUN?

HOW CAN YOU CARRY A GUN?

The main point to consider is that, in Arizona, a gun cannot be carried *concealed on yourself* in public unless you have a concealed-weapon permit. The top two pictures are legal only if you have a permit.

The law says it's not illegal to carry weapons:

"..in a belt holster which holster is wholly or partially visible," or:

"...in a scabbard or case designed for carrying weapons which scabbard or case is wholly or partially visible or carried in luggage."

Although the law *allows* weapons to be carried in a belt holster, it doesn't *require* that they be carried that way. A gun tucked in a belt or sticking out of a pocket violates no law, but is unsafe and not recommended.

In a car or other means of transportation, unless you have a concealed-weapon permit, you cannot conceal an unholstered gun within the immediate control of any person. You can have a gun anywhere in a car, loaded or unloaded, if it is in a case, holster or scabbard, or if it is in a storage compartment, trunk, pack, luggage or glove compartment, or if it is in plain sight.

With a concealed-weapon permit, there are no restrictions on how you may carry a gun on your person.

Special conditions for minors, guns on school grounds and guns in restricted places are detailed in Chapter 1.

GUN SAFETY AND
Concealed Weapon Training 5

Many fine books and classes exist which teach the current wisdom on gun safety and use. In Arizona, some of the best public classes are given by the Arizona Game and Fish Department and the Arizona State Rifle and Pistol Association, both listed in Appendix C.

When studying firearm safety (and every gun owner should), you will no doubt come across the Ten Commandments of Gun Safety. These well-intentioned lists have serious drawbacks—no two lists are ever the same and there are many more than ten rules to follow for safe gun use. In addition, hunters must learn many rules which don't apply to other shooters. For instance, a hunter should never openly carry game—it makes you an unwitting target of other hunters.

The Commandments of Safety are actually a way of saying, "Here's how people have accidents with guns." Each rule implies a kind of mishap. It's good exercise to look at each rule and read between the lines to find its counterpart— the potential disaster the rule will help you avoid. For example, rule number 1 translates into, "People have accidents with guns which they think are empty." Always keep in mind the prime directive: Take time to be safe instead of forever being sorry.

Carrying a concealed weapon in Arizona requires special training, testing and a permit issued by the Department of Public Safety. Information and questions for review by permit applicants appear after the safety rules.

THE GUN OWNER'S COMMANDMENTS OF SAFETY

1–Treat every gun as if it is loaded until you have personally proven otherwise.

2–Always keep a gun pointed in a safe direction.

3–Don't touch the trigger until you're ready to fire.

4–Be certain of your target and what is beyond it before pulling the trigger.

5–Keep a gun you carry holstered or concealed unless you're ready to use it.

6–Use but never rely on the safety.

7–Never load a gun until ready to use. Unload a gun immediately after use.

8–Only use ammunition which exactly matches the markings on your gun.

9–Always read and follow manufacturers' instructions carefully.

10–At a shooting range, always keep a gun pointed downrange.

11–Always obey a range officer's commands immediately.

12–Always wear adequate eye and ear protection when shooting.

13–If a gun fails to fire: a) keep it pointed in a safe direction; b) wait thirty seconds in case of a delayed firing; c) unload the gun carefully, avoiding exposure to the breech.

14–Don't climb fences or trees, or jump logs or ditches with a chambered round.

15–Be able to control the direction of the muzzle even if you stumble.

16–Keep the barrel and action clear of obstructions.

17–Avoid carrying ammunition which doesn't match the gun you are carrying.

18–Be aware that customized guns may require ammunition which doesn't match the gun's original markings.

19–Store guns with the action open.

20–Store ammunition and guns separately, and out of reach of children and careless adults.

21–Never pull a gun toward you by the muzzle.

22–Never horseplay with a firearm.

23–Never shoot at a hard flat surface, or at water, to prevent ricochets.

24–Be sure you have an adequate backstop for target shooting.

25–On open terrain with other people present, keep guns pointed upwards, or downwards and away from the people.

26–Never handle a gun you are not familiar with.

27–Learn to operate a gun empty before attempting to load and shoot it.

28–Never transport a loaded firearm in a vehicle.

29–Never lean a firearm where it may slip and fall.

30–Do not use alcohol or mood-altering drugs when you are handling firearms.

31–When loading or unloading a firearm, always keep the muzzle pointed in a safe direction.

32–Never use a rifle scope instead of a pair of binoculars.

33–Always remember that removing the magazine (sometimes called the clip) from semi-automatic and automatic weapons may still leave a live round, ready to fire, in the chamber.

34–Never rely on one empty cylinder next to the barrel of a revolver as a guarantee of safety, since different revolvers rotate in opposite directions.

35–Never step into a boat holding a loaded firearm.

36–It's difficult to use a gun safely until you become a marksman.

37–It's difficult to handle a gun safely if you need corrective lenses and are not wearing them.

38–Know the effective range and the maximum range of a firearm and the ammunition you are using.

39–Be sure that anyone with access to a firearm kept in a home understands its safe use.

40–Don't fire a large caliber weapon if you cannot control the recoil.

41–Never put your finger in the trigger guard when drawing a gun from a holster.

42–Never put your hand in front of the cylinder of a revolver when firing.

43–Never put your hand in back of the slide of a semi-automatic pistol when firing.

44–Always leave the hammer of a revolver resting over an empty chamber.

45–Never leave ammunition around when cleaning a gun.

46–Clean firearms after they have been used. A dirty gun is not as safe as a clean one.

47–Never fire a blank round directly at a person. Blanks can blind, maim, and at close range, they can kill.

48–Only use modern firearms in good working condition, and ammunition which is fresh.

49–Accidents don't happen, they are caused, and it's up to you and you alone to prevent them in all cases. Every "accident" which ever happened could have been avoided. Where there are firearms there is a need for caution.

50–Always think first and shoot second.

The Eddie Eagle Safety Rules for Kids—If you find a gun:
STOP! Don't touch. Leave the area. Tell an adult.

It is the responsibility
of every American
to prevent firearms from being
instruments of tragedy.

HOW WELL DO YOU KNOW YOUR GUN?

Safe and effective use of firearms demands that you understand your weapon thoroughly. This knowledge is best gained through a combination of reading, classes and practice with a qualified instructor. The simple test below will help tell you if you are properly trained in the use of firearms. If you're not sure what all the terms mean, can you be absolutely sure that you're qualified to handle firearms safely?

- ☐ Action
- ☐ Ammunition
- ☐ Automatic
- ☐ Ballistics
- ☐ Barrel
- ☐ Black powder
- ☐ Bolt
- ☐ Bore
- ☐ Break action
- ☐ Breech
- ☐ Buckshot
- ☐ Bullet
- ☐ Butt
- ☐ Caliber
- ☐ Cartridge
- ☐ Case
- ☐ Casing
- ☐ Centerfire
- ☐ Chamber
- ☐ Checkering
- ☐ Choke
- ☐ Clip
- ☐ Cock
- ☐ Comb
- ☐ Cylinder
- ☐ Discharge
- ☐ Dominant eye
- ☐ Effective range
- ☐ Firearm
- ☐ Firing Pin
- ☐ Firing Line
- ☐ Forearm
- ☐ Fouling
- ☐ Frame
- ☐ Gauge
- ☐ Grip
- ☐ Grip panels
- ☐ Grooves
- ☐ Gunpowder
- ☐ Half cock
- ☐ Hammer
- ☐ Handgun
- ☐ Hangfire
- ☐ Hunter orange
- ☐ Ignition
- ☐ Kneeling
- ☐ Lands
- ☐ Lever action
- ☐ Magazine
- ☐ Mainspring
- ☐ Maximum range
- ☐ Misfire
- ☐ Muzzle
- ☐ Muzzleloader
- ☐ Pattern
- ☐ Pistol
- ☐ Powder
- ☐ Primer
- ☐ Projectile
- ☐ Prone
- ☐ Pump action
- ☐ Pyrodex
- ☐ Receiver
- ☐ Repeater
- ☐ Revolver rifle
- ☐ Rifling
- ☐ Rimfire
- ☐ Safety
- ☐ Sear
- ☐ Semi-automatic
- ☐ Shell
- ☐ Shooting positions
- ☐ Shot
- ☐ Shotgun
- ☐ Sights
- ☐ Sighting-in
- ☐ Sitting
- ☐ Smokeless powder
- ☐ Smoothbore
- ☐ Standing
- ☐ Stock
- ☐ Trigger
- ☐ Trigger guard
- ☐ Unplugged shotgun

CONCEALED-WEAPON TRAINING

Arizona requires its concealed-weapon-permit holders to study legal issues related to firearms, use of deadly force and more (see chapter 1 for details), and to pass written and marksmanship tests in order to qualify for the permit.

Because the written test contents are determined solely by the approved training organizations (within the scope of the law), no standardized set of test questions exists. The course-content outline the Department of Public Safety provides to training organizations (summarized in chapter 1) serves as a basis for developing test questions.

Most of the outline areas focus on firearms, but it could be argued that the most critical part of the training concerns the use of deadly force, self-defense issues, confrontation avoidance and similar topics.

Some instructors logically point out that knowledge of the course contents cannot be tested in a ten-question exam, and require their students to take longer tests, showing a greater command of the material. Such courses exceed the state-mandated minimums and may be more difficult to pass, but provide you with an enhanced training opportunity. Here are sample test questions that CCW-permit applicants could reasonably be expected to know.

Areas of Study

1–Where are firearms prohibited in Arizona?
   (At least eleven places, study chapter 1)

2–What are the possible penalties for improper display of a weapon?
   (At least seven possible charges could be brought, study chapter 4)

3–What risks exist in drawing a firearm in public?
   (Could be used to justify a self-defense claim by another party, accidental discharge, discharge in prohibited area, more, study chapter 4)

4–When does state law justify the use of deadly force?
(Sixteen circumstances are described, study chapter 4)

5–What factors mitigate the strict legal definitions for justifiable use of deadly force?
(This is a complex issue frequently subject to debate and interpretation, fact-intensive and specific to the circumstances, study chapters 4, 5, and other books, such as In The Gravest Extreme, *by Massad Ayoob)*

6–What responsibility does a shooter have for shots fired which miss the intended target?
(Severe liabilities and penalties can result from the effect of stray bullets, study chapters 3 and 4)

7–Can you bring a firearm into a bar?
(Usually prohibited, but certain exceptions apply, study chapter 1)

8–What types of weapons are illegal?
(For federal- and state-law restrictions, study chapter 2)

9–Who can legally bear arms in Arizona?
(Age, residency, background, mental condition and more are taken into account, study chapter 1)

10–Under what circumstances can minors bear arms?
(Study chapters 1 and 4)

11–How can firearms be carried throughout the state?
(Different rules apply for yourself, in vehicles, while hunting, for minors and in school zones, study chapters 1 and 4)

12– What are the requirements for getting a CCW permit?
(Personal background, training and testing are involved, study chapters 1 and 5)

13–What do you have to do to ship firearms or carry them with you on a train, plane, or as you travel by car?
(Federal regulations control transit, study chapter 1)

14–How remote do you have to be to practice target shooting outdoors?
(Land office rules are plentiful, study chapter 3)

15–How much judgment is involved in deciding whether you can use deadly force in a situation?
(No easy answers to this, read everything you can find on the subject, study chapters 4 and 5, and recognize

that in using deadly force you accept very definite and substantial legal risks.)

16–What are the main rules of firearm safety?
(More than 50 exist, study chapter 5.)

17–What types of weapons are suitable for self-defense, and what are the best choices for you?
(A very important topic, not covered in this book, you should discuss this at length with your instructor.)

18–How do the various types of firearms operate?
(This topic should be covered by your instructor.)

19–What are the options for carrying a concealed weapon?
(This topic should be covered by your instructor.)

20–Have any new laws passed that you should know about?
(This requires ongoing information and vigilance.)

21–Are you mentally prepared to use deadly force?
(Mental conditioning for the use of deadly force is a required course component, and one that is not easily addressed. Until a moment arrives you may never truly know the answer to this question.)

As you can see, your preparation for carrying a concealed weapon can go well beyond the state-required minimums. Make the smart choice and exceed the minimum training by reading extensively, practicing regularly, keeping up on the important issues, and taking additional training programs.

Practice Test Questions

Approved CCW-training organizations develop a set of test questions which are reviewed and approved for permit-applicants' exams by the Department of Public Safety. The questions presented here are designed for study—to challenge your understanding, provoke thought and encourage discussion. Some of these have obvious yes-no or true-false answers, while others require a deeper understanding of the issues and must be answered with "maybe" or "it depends." Some defy clear answers. If you have trouble with any of these, ask your firearms safety instructor (and not the publisher!) for assistance.

1–Is it legal to point an empty gun at a person?

2–Is it legal to point an empty gun at anything?

3–Is it legal to put a gun in your pocket if you have a permit?

4–Is home defense with a machine gun legal?

5–Never tell family you keep a loaded gun in the house.

6–Always tell family you keep a loaded gun in the house.

7–Arizona requires you to lock your guns in a safe.

8–Arizona requires you to put a trigger lock on your guns.

9–Does the law say you may kill if your life is in danger?

10–Does the law say you may kill if your friend is in danger?

11–If a peace officer is in danger may you shoot to kill?

12–You may conceal weapons in Arizona without a permit.

13–You can't conceal weapons in Arizona without a permit.

14–A CCW permit prohibits concealing a bayonet.

15–A CCW permit prohibits bringing a gun onto a plane.

16–A CCW permit prohibits concealing explosives.

17–It's always illegal to bring a gun into a bar.

18–A bar's owner may carry a handgun in the bar.

19–A bar owner may allow the employees to be armed.

20–A bar owner may allow patrons to be armed.

21–Drawing a gun to settle a severe argument is legal.

22–Drawing a gun wrongly may lead to criminal charges.

23–Drawing a gun wrongly is permissible if you don't shoot.

24–If someone else draws a gun you may too.

25–If your life is immediately at risk you may draw a gun.

26–May you draw a gun to stop a serious crime in progress?

27–May you draw a gun to stop a kidnapping?

28–May you draw a gun to stop a robbery?

29–May you draw a gun to stop an armed robbery?

30–May you draw a gun to stop a sexual assault?

31–May you draw a gun to stop child molestation?

32–May you draw a gun to stop a serious traffic violation?

33–May you draw a gun to stop criminal trespass?

34–May you draw a gun to stop an arsonist?

35–May you draw a gun to stop vandals?

36–May you draw a gun to stop a first degree escape?

37–May you draw a gun to stop shoplifting?

38–May you shoot in items 25 through 37 above?

39–Do you want to ever have to shoot someone?

40–All states treat self-defense shooting the same way.

41–Federal law guarantees your rights no matter what.

42–Shooting criminals is legal if they are "in the act."

43–You should declare you have a CCW permit to police.

44–Never mention your CCW permit unless asked.

45–It's OK to let a concealed weapon show occasionally.

46–If you shoot a criminal you don't have to report it.

47–You should report any shooting incident to authorities.

48–If you shoot a criminal leave the body where it falls.

49–If you shoot a criminal outside your home drag him inside.

50–You're normally aware of everything around you.

51–When danger lurks, your awareness always goes up.

52–Even if you're cautious, danger can surprise you.

53–When you're surprised you're not always predictable.

54–Acting under stress can lead to surprising responses.

55–Name the four modes of mental awareness.

56–Describe the four modes of mental awareness.

57–The only official way to shoot is the Weaver stance.

58–You must grip a firearm with both hands to be legal.

59–Any shooting position you like is legal for self-defense.

60–If you pass your CCW exam you're perfectly qualified.

61–A CCW permit increases your personal safety.

62–A CCW permit increases your ability to respond.

63–A CCW permit will allow you to take back the streets.

64–With a CCW permit you may go wherever you want.

65–If a man charges you with a knife may you shoot him?

66–If a man charges you with a bat may you shoot him?

67–If a woman charges you with a bat may you shoot her?

68–If a man hits your spouse with a bat may you shoot him?

69–If a man threatens you with a bat may you shoot him?

70–If a man enrages you for no reason may you shoot him?

71–If a man won't let you get gasoline may you change his mind by drawing a gun?

72–If someone starts shooting someone else, may you shoot the first person to stop the attack?

73–Methods for controlling a violent confrontation are something that cannot be learned.

74–Will you need a gun more after you have a CCW permit than you did before you had a permit?

75–Have you ever witnessed a serious crime, such as a kidnapping, armed robbery or murder?

76–Are you more likely to witness a serious crime once you have a CCW permit?

77–Is it a good idea to qualify in your CCW marksmanship test with the same gun you plan on carrying regularly?

78–Unless you need to use it in an emergency, you should never let a concealed weapon show.

79–If you sell a gun to a person who uses it to commit a crime can you be charged with a crime?

80–What happens if you are found in Arizona with an unregistered handgun in your possession?

81–What is the legal maximum distance for a self-defense shooting in Arizona?

82–Arizona has preemption, which means that cities and counties may pass their own gun laws.

83–Many cities in Arizona have different gun laws that you must know and follow.

84–Many locations in Arizona interpret the laws differently and are allowed to do so by their courts.

85–What is a "citizens arrest," how do you make one, and is it a good idea to make one if you witness a crime?

86–If you see a drug deal going down, may you draw your gun and use deadly force to stop it?

87–If you see a prostitute operating in your neighborhood, may you threaten deadly force, without using it, to make the person leave?

88–If you use a gun legitimately to defend yourself there is a possibility you will be charged with a serious offense.

89–Many people who are charged with murder claim self-defense or accidental discharge.

90–Many people who use deadly force in self-defense are charged with murder.

91–The person who survives a lethal confrontation is often referred to as the defendant by the authorities.

92–If someone starts hitting you that's justification for threatening to use deadly force.

93–If someone starts hitting you that's justification for using deadly force.

94–If someone says they're going to start hitting you that's justification for threatening to use deadly force.

95–If someone hits you repeatedly in the face until you're bleeding, and then stops, you may draw your gun and shoot the attacker.

96–If someone comes into your place of business and commits a robbery, may you respond with deadly force?

97–A man says he's going to shoot you and sticks his hand in his pocket. May you shoot him first?

98–A woman says she's going to shoot you and sticks her

hand in her pocketbook. May you shoot her first?

99–If you are armed may you operate as a free-lance police officer?

100–The police may use deadly force in certain situations that you may not.

101–Tactics refers to the steps you take in an emergency.

102–Strategy refers to the plans you make in the event you are ever in an emergency.

103–A good crime avoidance plan includes tactics and strategy.

104–"Shoot first and ask questions later," is bad advice for personal self-defense.

105–It's always better to not shoot someone if you can safely avoid it.

106–If you get a CCW permit, does that change anything with respect to the number and seriousness of the threats you normally face in your daily routine?

107–Why does it make sense for you personally to get a concealed weapon permit?

108–Spending regular practice time on a shooting range after you get a CCW permit is a good idea.

In addition to questions such as the ones presented here, CCW applicants should study material and be able to answer questions on topics not covered in *The Arizona Gun Owner's Guide*, such as:

What are the various types of firearms, what are their component parts, and how do they operate; what are the various types of ammunition; what are the criteria for selecting a self-defense weapon and ammunition; what are the options for holsters and carrying weapons; how can you reduce the chances of unintentional firing and what are the primary firearm safety rules; what affects aiming and firing accurately; how should guns and ammunition be stored; how are guns cleaned, lubricated and checked, what are the tactics and strategies for personal self-defense and having weapons accessible; what alternatives are there to confrontation; how can threatening situations be managed; how can confrontations be avoided.

JUDGMENTAL SHOOTING

Concealed-weapon-permit holders are required to study issues related to judgmental shooting. The decision to use deadly force is rarely a clear-cut choice. Regardless of your familiarity with the laws, your degree of training, the quality of your judgmental skills and your physical location and condition at the time of a deadly threat, the demands placed on you at the critical moment are as intense as anything you will normally experience in your life, and your actual performance is an unknown.

Every situation is different. The answers to many questions relating to deadly force are subject to debate. To be prepared for armed response you must recognize that such situations are not black or white, and that your actions, no matter how well intentioned, will be evaluated by others, probably long after you act. The chances that you will come away from a lethal encounter without any scars—legal, physical or psychological—are small, and the legal risks are substantial. That's why it's usually best to practice prevention and avoidance rather than confrontation, whenever possible.

Most people can think about it this way: You've gotten along this far in life without ever having pulled a concealed weapon on someone, much less having fired it. The odds of that changing once you have a CCW permit are about the same—practically zero. A concealed weapon may make you feel more secure, but it doesn't change how safe your surroundings actually are, in the places you normally travel, one bit. And it certainly isn't safe to think of a concealed weapon as a license (or a talisman) for walking through potentially dangerous areas you would otherwise avoid like the plague.

Remember that the person holding a gun after a shooting is frequently thought of as the bad guy—the perpetrator—even if it's you and you acted in self-defense. The person who is shot has a different, more sympathetic name—the victim—and gets the benefit of a prosecutor even if, perhaps, you learn later its a hardened criminal with a long record. Maybe your defense will improve if it is indeed a serious repeat offender, but you won't know that until after the fact, and don't count on it. If you ever have to raise a gun to a criminal, you'll find out quickly how good they can be at portraying you as the bad guy and themselves as the helpless innocents, at the mercy of a crazed wacko—you.

Situational Analysis

Think about the deadly force encounters described below, and consider discussing them with your CCW trainer:

1–If you are being seriously attacked by a man with a club, is it legal for you to aim for his leg so you can stop the attack without killing him?

2–If you enter your home and find a person looting your possessions are you justified in shooting to kill?

3–If you enter your home and find a person looting your possessions, who runs out the back door as he hears you arrive, can you shoot him to keep him from escaping?

4–If you enter your home and find a person looting your possessions, who turns and whirls toward you when you enter, literally scaring you to death, may you shoot to kill and expect to be justified?

5–If you enter your home and find a stranger in it who charges you with a knife, may you shoot to kill?

6–A stranger in your home has just stabbed your spouse and is about to stab your spouse again. May you shoot the stranger from behind to stop the attack?

7–As you walk past a park at night you notice a woman tied to a tree and a man tearing off her clothing. May you use deadly force to stop his actions?

8–A police officer is bleeding badly and chasing a man in prison coveralls who runs right past you. May you shoot the fleeing suspect while he is in close range to you?

9–You're in your home at night when a man with a ski mask on comes through an open window in the hallway. May you shoot to kill?

10–You're in your home at night, sleeping, when a noise at the other end of the house awakens you. Taking your revolver you quietly walk over to investigate and notice a short person going through your silverware drawer, 45 feet from where you're standing. The person doesn't notice you. May you shoot to kill?

11–As you approach your parked car in a dark and remote section of a parking lot, three youthful toughs approach you from three separate directions. You probably can't unlock your vehicle and get in before they reach you, and you're carrying a gun. What should you do?

12–From outside a convenience store you observe what clearly appears to be an armed robbery—four people are being held at gunpoint while the store clerk is putting money into a paper bag. You're armed. What should you do?

13-You're waiting to cross the street in downtown and a beggar asks you for money. He's insistent and begins to insult you when you refuse to ante up. Finally he gets loud and belligerent and says he'll kill you if you don't give him ten dollars. Can you shoot him?

14–You get in your car, roll down the windows, and before you can drive off a man sticks a knife in the window and orders you to get out. Can you shoot him?

15–You get in your car, and before you start it a man points a gun at you and tells you to get out. You have gun in the pocket on the door, another under the seat, and a gun in a holster in your pants. What should you do?

16–Before you get in your car, a man with a gun comes up from behind, demands your car keys, takes them, and while holding you at gun point, starts your car and drives away. Can you shoot at him while he's escaping?

17–You're walking to your car in the mall parking lot after a movie when two armed hoods jump out of a shadow and demand your money. You've got a gun in your back pocket. What should you do?

18–A masked person with a gun stops you on the street, demands and takes your valuables, and then flees down the street on foot. You're carrying a concealed firearm. What should you do?

19–A youngster runs right by you down the street, and an old lady shouts, "Stop him, he killed my husband!" Can you shoot to stop his getaway?

20–You're at work when two ornery-looking dudes amble in. You can smell trouble, so you walk to a good vantage point behind a showcase. Sure enough, they pull guns and announce a stick-up. You and your four employees are armed and there are several customers in the store. What's your move?

21–Your friend and you have been drinking, and now you're arguing over a football bet. You say the spread was six points, he says four. There's $500 hanging in the balance of a five point game, and it represents your mortgage payment. He pulls a knife and says, "Pay me or I'll slice you up." You've got a gun in your pocket. What should you do?

22–At a gas station, the lines are long, it's hot, and the guy next in line starts getting surly. You're not done pumping and he hits you in the face and tells you to finish up. He shuts off your pump and says he'll kick your butt if you don't move on. Should you pull your gun to put him in his place?

Observations about the situations presented:

1–The justification to use deadly force is never justification to intentionally wound.

2–Not enough information is provided to make an informed choice.

3–No. The penalty for burglary is jail, not death, and you almost never have the right to kill to prevent a criminal from escaping. Once the danger to you is over—and it is once the criminal is fleeing—your right to use deadly force ends.

4–Probably. But do you always enter your home prepared for mortal combat? Does your story have holes a prosecutor will notice?

5–It's hard to imagine not being justified in this situation, but stranger things have happened.

6–It's hard to imagine not being justified in this situation, but stranger things have happened. Will the bullet exit the attacker and wound your spouse?

7–Not necessarily, since you don't know if the people are consenting adults who like this sort of thing. A seasoned peace officer might cautiously approach the couple, weapon drawn, and with words instead of force determine what's happening, and then make further choices depending on the outcome.

8–Probably not, under existing state law (see §13-410) and under recent court rulings about civilians shooting at fleeing suspects, but if the officer enlists your aid (see §13-2403), possibly yes.

9–Probably, though a well-trained expert might instead confront the intruder from a secure position and succeed in holding the person for arrest, which is no easy task. Armed and from good cover, you might also convince the intruder to leave the way he came.

10–Perhaps, but the distance and lack of immediate threat will make for a difficult explanation when the police arrive, and if the perpetrator has an accomplice that you didn't notice, the danger to you is severe. If the perpetrator turns out to be a thief with a long rap sheet, you might not even be charged. If it turns out that the intruder is 11 years old your court defense will be extremely difficult. Remember, you're obligated to not shoot if you don't absolutely have to. Has your training prepared you for this?

11–That's a good question, and you should never have parked there in the first place.

12–Call for assistance, go to a defensible position, continue to observe, and recognize that charging into such a volatile situation is incredibly risky for all parties.

13–You are never justified in using deadly force in response to verbal provocation alone, no matter how severe.

14–The prosecutor will make it clear that if you could have stepped on the gas and escaped, the threat to you would have ended, and the need to shoot did not exist. If you were boxed into a parking space, the need to defend yourself would be hard for a prosecutor to refute. These things often come down to the exact circumstances and the quality of the attorneys.

15–Get out quietly and don't provoke someone who has the drop on you. All your guns are no match for a drawn weapon. This is where a real understanding of tactics comes into play.

16–No. You are almost never justified in shooting at an escaping criminal. The penalty for grand theft auto is jail time, not death. Once the threat to you is over, so is the justification for using lethal force.

17–Not enough information is provided to make an informed choice.

18–Nothing, though you could chase him, but it's extremely unwise and risky to you. You are almost never justified in shooting at an escaping criminal (kidnapping, under certain circumstances, might be an exception). The penalty for armed robbery is jail time, not death. Once the threat to you is over, so is the justification for using lethal force. Anyone crazy enough to rob you at gunpoint must be considered capable of doing anything, and the smart move is to avoid further confrontation and stay alive.

19–You don't have enough information. When in doubt don't shoot.

20–This is where strategy and tactics are critical. If you allow your employees to carry and are prepared for armed defense of your premises you better get plenty of advanced training in gunfighting and self-defense. You'll need it to survive, and you'll need it to meet the legal challenges later. If a customer gets shot by one of your own, even if you get the villains, you're in for big time trouble and grief. If no one gets hurt but the criminals, you'll be a hero. Either outcome remains burned in memory. Tough choice.

21–Too many killings occur between people who know each other. Your chance of a successful legal defense in a case like this are remote. Would he have really killed you? Probably not. Did you have any other options besides killing him? Probably so. Have you fought like this before? Maybe. What would the witnesses say? Nothing you could count on, and probably all the wrong things. The fact that you have a firearm and can use it doesn't mean you should, the likelihood of absolutely having to use it are small, and using it to settle a bet with a friend over a point spread may not be the worst thing you can do but it's close.

22–Cap your tank and move on, you don't need the grief. Or go into the station and tell them what's happened, preparing yourself mentally for further hostilities. Go to a defensible position and call the police. Avoid a confrontation at all costs. See what the other guy does before you do anything. Decide to take another course in how to handle volatile situations and difficult people. And realize that the fact that you have a CCW permit and a lot of training doesn't solve any problems or reduce your risks in life.

RECOMMENDED READING

Knowledge is power, and the more you have the better off you are likely to be. Some CCW trainers will require that you read important books on personal safety, crime avoidance, self-defense and the use of deadly force. **Whether your instructor requires it or not, decide to read about this critical subject.** A selection of some of the most highly regarded books on these topics appears at the back of *The Arizona Gun Owner's Guide* and are easily available directly from the publisher. If your instructor doesn't include these in your course, get them yourself. The single best book on the subject is probably *In The Gravest Extreme*, by Massad Ayoob.

You may also choose to obtain a complete copy of the Arizona criminal code, since the laws reproduced in *The Arizona Gun Owner's Guide* are a selected excerpt of gun laws only. Remember that no published edition of the law is complete without the legislation passed during the most recent session of the state congress, and that federal laws may be passed at any time. An annotated edition of the law, available in major libraries, provides critical information in the form of court cases which clarify and expand on the meaning of the actual statutes.

APPENDIX A
GLOSSARY OF TERMS

Words, when used in the law, often have special meanings you wouldn't expect from simply knowing the English language. For the complete legal description of these and other important terms, see each chapter of the criminal code and other legal texts dealing with language. The following plain English descriptions are provided for your convenience only.

ACT—A bodily movement.

ADEQUATE PROVOCATION—Conduct or circumstances sufficient to make a reasonable person lose self-control.

ARREST—To deprive a person of liberty by legal authority.

B•B GUN—A gun designed to forcibly propel a ball, pellet, dart or other projectile using compressed gas or a spring mechanism.

BENEFIT—Anything of value or advantage, now or in the future.

BIG GAME—Antelope, bear, bison (buffalo), deer, elk, mountain lion, peccary (javelina), bighorn sheep and wild turkey.

CONDUCT—The actions you take or refrain from, and your thoughts about them.

CRIME—A felony or misdemeanor.

CRIMINAL NEGLIGENCE—Failure to recognize a risk so dangerous that a reasonable person would be expected to recognize it.

CULPABLE MENTAL STATE—An accountable state of mind. Specifically: intentionally, knowingly, recklessly or with criminal negligence, in the senses described by law.

DANGEROUS DRUG—For a detailed description, see Arizona Revised Statutes, 13-3401.

DANGEROUS INSTRUMENT—Anything which can readily be used to cause death or serious physical in jury.

DEADLY PHYSICAL FORCE—Force which can cause death or serious physical injury.

DEADLY WEAPON—Anything designed for lethal use. The term

includes a firearm.

DEAL—To engage in the business of selling firearms at wholesale or to repair or modify firearms, with the principal objective of making a livelihood or profit.

DEFACE—To remove, alter or destroy the manufacturer's serial number.

ENTERPRISE—A corporation, association, labor union or other legal entity.

EXPLOSIVE—Dynamite, nitroglycerine, black powder, plastic explosive or other similar materials. Ammunition and hand-loading ammunition supplies are excluded.

FELONY—A serious crime. An offense against the law which carries a sentence of imprisonment under the custody of the state Department of Corrections. Felony prison sentences run from 6 months to life imprisonment with no chance of parole until 25 years have been served. A class 1 felony (1st degree murder) carries a possible sentence of death. Arizona uses the gas chamber or lethal injection to inflict the penalty of death. Felony fines may be up to $150,000 for an individual, and up to $1,000,000 for an enterprise.

FIREARM—Any loaded or unloaded handgun, pistol, revolver, rifle, shotgun or other weapon which can fire a projectile by using an explosive or expanding gasses. A permanently inoperable firearm is excluded.

GOVERNMENT—The recognized political structure.

GOVERNMENT FUNCTION—Any activity which a public servant is authorized to do for the government.

GUN—A firearm.

HOMICIDE—First or second degree murder, manslaughter or negligent homicide.

ILLEGAL—Unlawful. An offense. A crime.

INTENTIONALLY or WITH THE INTENT TO—With the objective of causing a specific result.

INTOXICATION—Mental or physical incapacity caused by drugs, toxic vapors or alcohol.

JUSTIFICATION—Legal right to use physical or deadly physical force.

KNOWINGLY—With awareness of your conduct and situation.

LAW—Formal rules by which society controls itself. In Arizona, the law means the Arizona Revised Statutes. Cities and other governments within the state may not enact a law which contradicts state law.

LESSEE—A person who leases something from another person.

MACHINE GUN—A firearm capable of shooting more than one shot automatically, by a single pull of the trigger.

MISDEMEANOR—A crime less serious than a felony. An offense against the law which carries a sentence of imprisonment in a local facility, not to the state Department of Corrections. Misdemeanor jail sentences run up to six months. Misdemeanor fines can run up to $2,500 for an individual, and up to $20,000 for an enterprise.

NARCOTIC DRUG—For a detailed description, see Arizona Revised Statutes, 13-3401.

OFFENSE—Any conduct described in the law which carries a jail sentence or fine. A crime.

OMISSION—Failure to do something required by law.

PEACE OFFICER—Anyone with legal authority to maintain public order and make arrests.

PERSON—A human being, or, as applicable, an enterprise or government.

PETTY OFFENSE—A minor criminal violation. An offense against the law which carries only a fine as a penalty. Petty offenses run up to $300 for an individual, and up to $1000 for an enterprise.

PHYSICAL FORCE—Force used on another person. Confining another person is considered physical force.

PHYSICAL INJURY—Harm to the physical condition of a person or property.

POACHING—Hunting illegally, by either hunting without a valid license, outside of regulations, taking wildlife during closed season or possessing unlawfully taken wildlife.

POSSESS—To knowingly have or exercise control over property.

POSSESSION—The voluntary act of exercising control over property.

PREMEDITATION—Acting with the intention or knowledge that you will kill another human being. The intention or knowledge must precede the killing by a length of time sufficient to permit reflection. Killing in the instant effect of a sudden quarrel or heat of passion is not premeditation.

PROHIBITED POSSESSOR—A person who is not allowed to have a gun. See Chapter 1 for a detailed description.

PROHIBITED WEAPON—Guns and other weapons which are a crime to have, make, sell, transport or transfer without federal registration. A National Firearms Act (NFA) weapon. See Chapter 2 for a detailed description.

PROPERTY—Anything of tangible or intangible value.

PUBLIC SERVANT—Any officer or employee of any branch of government. Public servants may be elected, appointed, or hired. Consultants working for government and peace officers are included. You become a public servant at the time you are selected, which may be before you actually occupy the specific government position. Jurors and witnesses are excluded.

REASONABLE—This term is used to describe behavior and circumstances which fit into a generally recognized and accepted norm. It is frequently possible to argue about the precise meaning of the word, depending on the situation.

REASONABLE PERSON—An imaginary person who conforms to generally recognized and accepted norms.

RECKLESSLY—With awareness of and disregard for a risk so dangerous that a reasonable person would not ignore it.

RIFLED BARREL—A gun barrel with internal grooves for giving the bullet a spin which helps stabilize it in flight. Rifled weapons are restricted in limited areas, notably the Maricopa County Parks. Most handguns are rifled.

SERIOUS PHYSICAL INJURY—Injury which creates a reasonable risk of death. Also, injury which causes serious and permanent disfigurement, loss of any organ or limb, or serious long-term harm to health, an organ or a limb.

TAKING—Pursuing, shooting, hunting, fishing, trapping, killing, capturing, snaring or netting wildlife, or placing any device to capture or kill wildlife.

TRANSFER—Sell, assign, pledge, lease, loan, give away or otherwise dispose of.

UNLAWFUL—Against the law. Illegal. A crime.

VEHICLE—Any device used for transportation of people or property, on a road, waterway, airway or off-road. Devices using solely human power, and devices which travel on tracks or rails are excluded.

VOLUNTARY ACT—A deliberate bodily movement.

VOLUNTARY INTOXICATION—Getting drunk or high on alcohol, drugs or toxic vapors which you know, or should know, will cause the effect. Taking alcohol, drugs or toxic vapors under medical advice is excluded. Taking such substances under duress may afford a defense.

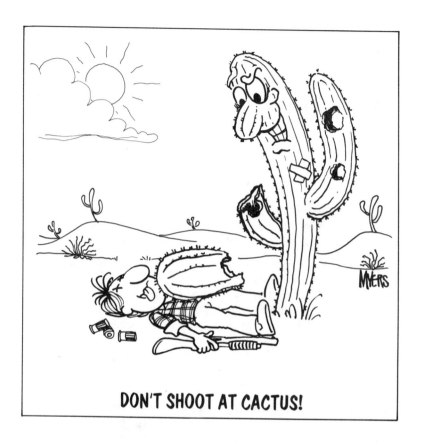

DON'T SHOOT AT CACTUS!

Cactus is a treasure which the state of Arizona is lucky to have. They are legally protected plants—it's a crime to shoot at them or harm them in any way. Removing any cactus from the desert without special authorization is against the law. Only the lowest and sleaziest dregs of society would even think of shooting at these harmless and majestic natives of the state.

Cactus can't shoot back, but there's at least one case on record of a cactus that got even! (The scene depicted actually occurred on February 4, 1982, just west of Lake Pleasant in Maricopa County, when a man was crushed to death by a 23-foot section of the saguaro cactus he had been shooting with rifled slugs from a 16-gauge shotgun.)

APPENDIX B
Crime and Punishment Chart

EXPLANATIONS

Type of Crime: Illegal activities are divided into these ten categories, to match the punishment to the crime. The category may be effected by how the crime is committed.

Jail Term: These are the ranges for a first offense involving a gun; many crimes have special sentences. The back cover shows maximum sentences for first offense without a gun. A class 1 felony, in addition to life imprisonment with no chance of parole for at least 25 years, carries a possible death penalty for first degree murder, which is administered by lethal injection or the gas chamber. Sentences may be raised or lowered, based on circumstances, involving court discretion, and using guidelines set out in chapter 7 of the state criminal code.

Fines: These are maximums, which may be lowered at court discretion. Fines are payable immediately, but a court may grant permission to pay by a certain date or in installments.

Statute of Limitations: The period of time, from the discovery of an offense (or from the time when an offense should have been discovered with the exercise of reasonable diligence), within which a prosecution may begin. When a class 2, 3 or 4 felony involves homicide there is no time limit. The period of limitation is put on hold if you are out of state, or if you have no known abode within the state. Plea bargaining a class 6 felony to a misdemeanor does not change the time limit.

Offenses: This is a partial list and exceptions often apply. For example, sexual assault with a gun carries life imprisonment with no chance of parole for at least 25 years.

CRIME AND PUNISHMENT

Type of Crime	Jail Term 1st Offense	Max. Fine for Person	Max. Fine for Business	Statute of Limitation
Class 1 Felony	**For Life**	**$150,000**	**$1 Million**	**None**

First degree murder, second degree murder.

Class 2 Felony	**4–10 Yrs.**	**$150,000**	**$1 Million**	**7 Years**

Attempted murder, armed robbery, bringing a gun into a prison, drive by shooting, kidnapping, sexual conduct with minor under 15, sexual assault, child molestation, first degree burglary of residence, arson of occupied structure, promoting prison contraband.

Class 3 Felony	**2.5–7 Yrs.**	**$150,000**	**$1 Million**	**7 Years**

Manslaughter, assisting a suicide, aggravated assault, first degree burglary of non-residence, second degree burglary.

Class 4 Felony	**1.5–3 Yrs.**	**$150,000**	**$1 Million**	**7 Years**

Negligent homicide, possession or sale of a prohibited weapon, first degree escape, perjury, possession of a gun by a prohibited possessor.

Class 5 Felony	**.75–2 Yrs.**	**$150,000**	**$1 Million**	**7 Years**

Bringing a gun into or around a juvenile correctional facility, first degree hindering prosecution, second degree escape, obstructing criminal investigation, any unclassified felony in state law.

Class 6 Felony	**.5–1.5 Yrs.**	**$150,000**	**$1 Million**	**7 Years**

Transferring firearms to a minor without written consent from parent or guardian, endangerment with a risk of death, defacing a gun, possessing a defaced gun, providing a gun to a prohibited possessor, resisting arrest, third degree escape, unlawful sale of big game.

Class 1 Misdemeanor	**6 mos.**	**$2,500**	**$20,000**	**1 Year**

Concealing a weapon on yourself or in a car if you are not a permitee, refusing to leave or check deadly weapons at a public place or event when asked, entering a polling place on day of election armed, having firearm on school grounds, having firearm at nuclear plant, endangerment without a risk of death, threatening or intimidating, disorderly conduct, first degree criminal trespass, refusing to aid peace officer, poaching big game.

Class 2 Misdemeanor	**4 mos.**	**$750**	**$10,000**	**1 Year**

Shooting within city limits, bringing a gun into a bar, threatened assault, most hunting violations, carrying concealed weapon without carrying your valid permit, any unclassified misdemeanor in state law.

Class 3 Misdemeanor	**30 days**	**$500**	**$2,000**	**1 Year**

Failure to report gunshot wound, physically provoking someone, criminal nuisance.

Petty Offense	**None**	**$300**	**$1,000**	**1 Year**

Any offense not classified as a felony or misdemeanor.

APPENDIX C
THE PROPER AUTHORITIES

Regulations on guns and their use come from a lot of places. Listed with each authority are the addresses and phones of the nearest offices. All phone numbers are in area code (602) and all cities are in Arizona (AZ) unless indicated.

Arizona Commission on Indian Affairs 542-3123 1645 W. Jefferson, Phoenix 85007
    Ak-Chin Reservation, Ak-Chin Indian Community 568-2221
        Route 2, Box 27, Maricopa 85239
    Camp Verde Reservation, Yavapai-Apache Indian Community 567-3649
        P.O. Box 1188, Camp Verde 86322
    Cocopah Reservation, Cocopah Tribe 627-2102
        Bin G, Somerton 85350
    Colorado River Reservation, Colorado River Indian Tribes 669-9211
        Route 1, Box 23-B, Parker 85344
    Fort Apache Reservation, White Mountain Apache Tribe 338-4346
        P.O. Box 1150, Whiteriver 85941
    Fort McDowell Reservation, Mohave-Apache Tribe 990-0995
        P.O. Box 17779, Fountain Hills 85268
    Fort Mojave Reservation, Fort Mojave Tribe (619) 326-4591
        500 Merriman Avenue, Needles, CA 92363
    Fort Yuma Reservation, Quechan Tribe (619) 572-0213
        P. O. Box 11352, Yuma 85366
    Gila River Reservation, Gila River Indian Community 562-3311
        P.O. Box 97, Sacaton 85247
    Havasupai Reservation, Havasupai Tribe 448-2731, P.O. Box 10, Supai 86435
    Hopi Reservation, Hopi Tribe 734-2441, P.O. Box 123, Kyakotsmovi 86039
    Hualapai Reservation, Hualapai Tribe 769-2216
        P.O. Box 168, Peach Springs 86434
    Kaibab-Paiute Reservation, Kaibab-Paiute Tribe 643-7245
        Tribal Affairs Building, Fredonia 86022
    Navajo Reservation, The Navajo Tribe 871-4941
        P.O. Box 308, Window Rock 86515
    Pascua Yaqui Reservation, Pascua Yaqui Tribe 883-2838
        7474 S. Camino de Oeste, Tucson 85746
    Salt River Reservation, Salt River Pima-Maricopa Indian Community 941-7277
        Route 1, Box 216, Scottsdale 85256
    San Carlos Reservation, San Carlos Apache Tribe 475-2361
        P.O. Box "O", San Carlos 85550
    Tohono O'Odham Reservation, Tohono O'Odham Tribe 383-2221
        P.O. Box 837, Sells 85634
    Tonto Apache Reservation, Tonto Apache Tribe 474-5000
        #30 Tonto Apache Reservation, Payson 85547
    Yavapai-Prescott Reservation, Yavapai-Prescott Tribe 445-8790
        530 E. Merritt Street, Prescott 86301

Arizona Game and Fish Department (AGFD) 942-3000
    2222 West Greenway Road, Phoenix 85034
        AGFD Region 1 367-4342, HC 66, Box 57201, Pinetop 85935
        AGFD Region II 774-5045, 3500 S. Lake Mary Road, Flagstaff 86001
        AGFD Region III 692-7700, 5325 N. Stockton Hill Road, Kingman 86401
        AGFD Region IV 342-0091, 9140 E. County 10.5 St., Yuma 85365
        AGFD Region V 628-5376, 555 North Greasewood, Tucson 85745
        AGFD Region VI 981-9400, 7200 E. University, Mesa 85207
Arizona State Land Department 542-4621, 1616 W. Adams, Phoenix 85007
Arizona State Parks 542-4174, 800 W. Washington #415, Phoenix 85007
    Alamo Lake State Park 669-2088, 38 mi. north of Wenden and US 60
    Boyce Thompson SW Arboretum 689-2811, 3 mi. west of Superior on US 60
    Buckskin Mountain State Park 667-3231, 11 mi. north of Parker on AZ 95
    Catalina State Park 628-5798, 9 mi. north of Tucson on US 89
    Dead Horse Ranch State Park 634-5283, Across river from Cottonwood,
        Enter on north, 5th Street
    Fort Verde State Historic Park 567-3275, In Camp Verde, 3 mi. east of 1-17
    Homolovi Ruins State Park 289-4106, 5 mi. east of Winslow off Highway 87
    Jerome State Historic Park 634-5381, In Jerome, off US 89A
    Kartchner Caverns State Park, P.O. Box 1849, Benson
    Lake Havasu State Park Windsor Beach 855-7851, Off AZ 95, in Lake Havasu City
    Cattail Cove 855-1223, 15 mi. south of Lake Havasu City
    Lost Dutchman State Park 982-4485, 5 mi. northeast of Apache Junction on AZ 88
    Lyman Lake State Park 337-4441, 11 mi. south of St. Johns, 1 mi. east of US 666
    McFarland Historical State Park 868-5216, In Florence, off US 89 and AZ 287
    Oracle State Park 896-2425 1 mi. east of Oracle off the old Mt. Lemmon Rd.
    Painted Rocks State Park 683-2151, 15 mi. west and 12 mi. north of Gila Bend
    Patagonia Lake State Park 287-6965, 12 mi. northeast of Nogales on AZ 82
    Picacho Peak State Park 466-3183, 40 mi. north of Tucson on 1-10
    Red Rock State Park 282-6907 South of Sedona, off Red Rock Loop Rd.
    Riordan State Historic Park 779-4395 In Flagstaff, off Riordan Ranch St.
    Roper Lake State Park 428-6760, 6 mi. south of Safford, 1/2 mi. east of US 666
    Slide Rock State Park 282-3034 7 mi north of Sedona on 89A
    Tombstone Courthouse State, Historic Park 457-3311, In Tombstone, off US 80
    Tubac Presidio State Historic Park 398-2252 In Tubac. off 1-19
    Yuma Territorial Prison State Historic Park 783-4771, 343-2500 In Yuma, off 1-8
Arizona Handgun Permit Hotline (DPS) Phoenix 256-6280, statewide 1-800-256-6280
Arizona State Rifle and Pistol Association 838-6064, P.O. Box 40962, Mesa, AZ 85274
Bureau of Alcohol, Tobacco and, Firearms (202) 927-8410
    650 Massachusetts Avenue, NW, Washington, DC 20226
Bureau of Alcohol, Tobacco and Firearms, Arizona Office 640-2025, 2938, 2840
    201 E. Indianola, Phoenix 85012
Bureau of Indian Affairs (202) 208-7163, 1849 C. Street, NW, Washington, DC 20240
Bureau of Indian Affairs Arizona Office 379-6600
    1 N. 1st St., P.O. Box 10, Phoenix 85001
Bureau of Land Management (BLM) (202) 343-5717
    U.S. Dept. of Interior, 18th & C St. NW, Wash., DC 20240
    BLM Arizona State Office 650-0509 3707 N. 7th Street, Phoenix 85014
    BLM Arizona Strip Dist. Office (801) 673-3545 390 N. 3050 E., St. George, UT 84770
    BLM Havasu Resource Area Office 855-8017 3189 Sweetwater Avenue,
        Lake Havasu City 86403
    BLM Kingman Resource Area Office 757-3161 2475 Beverly Avenue, Kingman 86401
    BLM Phoenix District Office 780-8090 2015 W. Deer Valley Rd., Phoenix 85027
    BLM Safford District Office 428-4040 425 E. 4th Street, Safford 85546
    BLM Tucson District Office 722-4289 12661 E. Broadway, Tucson 85748
    BLM Yuma District Office 726-6300 3150 Winsor Avenue, Yuma 85365
County Parks and Recreation Departments (P&RD)
    Coconino County P&RD 779-5130 100 E. Birch, Flagstaff 86001
    Maricopa County P&RD 506-2930 3475 W. Durango, Phoenix 85009
    Mohave County P&RD 753-0739 P.O. Box 7000, Kingman 86401
    Navajo County P&RD 524-3094 P.O. Box 668. Holbrook 86025
    Pima County P&RD 740-2680 1204 W. Silver Lake Road, Tucson 85713
    Yavapai County P&RD 771-3321 County Courthouse, Room 107, Prescott 86301
Lawyer Referral 257-4434, 333 W. Roosevelt, Phoenix 85003
National Park Service 640-5250, 202 E. Earll #115, Phoenix 85012
    Canyon de Chelly National Monument 674-5436 Box 588, Chinle 86503
    Casa Grande Ruins National Monument 723-3172 1100 Ruins Drive, Coolidge 85228
    Chiracahua National Monument 824-3560 or 824-3460 Wilcox 85643

Glen Canyon National Recreation Area 645-2471 Box 1507, Paqe 86040
Grand Canyon National Park 638-7888 Box 129, Grand Canyon 86023
Lake Mead National Recreation Area (702) 293-8920 601 Nevada Highway,
    Boulder City, NV 89005
Montezuma Castle National Monument 567-3322 P.O. Box 219, Campe Verde 86322
Navajo National Monument 672-2366 Tonalea 86044
Organ Pipe Cactus National Monument 387-6849 Route 1, Box 100, Ajo 85321
Petrified Forest National Park 524-6228 Petrified Forest National Park 86028
Pipe Springs National Monument (801) 643-5505 c/o Zion National Park,
    Springdale, UT 84767
Saguaro National Monument 670-6680 Old Spanish Trail, Rt. 8, Box 695,
Tucson 85730
Sunset Crater National Monument 527-7042 Route 3, Box 149, Flagstaff 86004
Tonto National Monument 467-2241 Box 707, Roosevelt 85545
Tumacacori National Monument 398-2341 Box 67, Tumacacori 85640
Tuzigoot National Monument 634-5564 Box 219, Camp Verde 86322
Walnut Canyon National Monument 526-3367 Walnut Canyon Road, Flagstaff 86004
Wupatki National Monument 527-7040 HC 33, Box 444A, Flagstaff 86004
National Rifle Association (800) 336-7402
    1600 Rhode Island Avenue NW, Washington, DC 20036
National Rifle Association, Arizona (Cactus Match League) 831-0685
Secretary of State (Arizona) 542-4285, Publications 542-4086
    Capitol West Wing, Phoenix 85007
U.S. Forest Service Offices
    Forest Service, U.S. Dept. of, Agriculture, (202) 655-4000
        P.O. Box 96090, Washington, D.C. 20090
    Regional Forester (505) 842-3292
        Federal Bldg., 517 Gold Avenue,, Albuquerque, NM 87102
    Apache-Sitgreaves National Forest 333-4301,
        4372 S. Mountain Avenue, Hwy. 180, P.O. Box 640,, Springerville 85935
    Coconino National Forest 527-3600, 2323 E. Greenlaw Lane, Flagstaff 86001
    Coronado National Forest 670-4552, Federal Bldg., 300 W. Congress, Tucson 85701
    Kaibab National Forest 635-2681, 800 S. 6th St., Williams 86046
    Prescott National Forest 771-4700, 344 S. Cortez St., Prescott 86303
    Sitgreaves National Forest, Now consolidated with Apache National Forest
    Tonto National Forest 225-5200, 2324 E. McDowell. Phoenix 85010

APPENDIX D
THE ARIZONA GUN LAWS

On the following pages are excerpts from the Arizona Revised Statutes, Title 13, Criminal Code, electronically scanned from original Secretary of State documents, and cross-read proofed against the official Michie published edition (1993). New gun laws from the 1994 legislative session have been carefully added and proofed, making this the most comprehensive single edition currently available. Although this has been prepared with great care, no assurance of accuracy or completeness is made and for strict legal use official versions are recommended.

Title 13 covers all criminal conduct, but only gun laws for private citizens are included in this appendix. The blank spaces appearing in the appendix are to allow for future additions to the law. A complete copy of the Criminal Code is available in libraries, but keep in mind that those copies are incomplete (and in many instances inaccurate) without the relevant material from the 380 bills passed in 1994.

How State Law Is Arranged

Arizona's laws are covered under 46 separate "titles." Within each title, each piece of law is numbered, starting at 101, and going as high as necessary. Each numbered part is called a "section," represented by a "§" sign. This makes it easy to refer to any particular law—just call it by its title and section numbers. For instance, §13-3102 is the part about misconduct with weapons. You say it like this, "title thirteen, section thirty one oh two," or simply, "thirteen thirty one oh two."

Excerpt from the Constitution of the State of Arizona

Section 26. Bearing Arms. The right of the individual citizen to bear arms in defense of himself or the state shall not be impaired, but nothing in this section shall be construed as authorizing individuals or corporations to organize, maintain, or employ an armed body of men.

EXCERPTS FROM THE ARIZONA REVISED STATUTES
TITLE 13 • CRIMINAL CODE

CHAPTER 1 • GENERAL PROVISIONS

13-101. Purposes

It is declared that the public policy of this state and the general purposes of the provisions of this title are:

1. To proscribe conduct that unjustifiably and inexcusably causes or threatens substantial harm to individual or public interests;

2. To give fair warning of the nature of the conduct proscribed and of the sentences authorized upon conviction;

3. To define the act or omission and the accompanying mental state which constitute each offense and limit the condemnation of conduct as criminal when it does not fall within the purposes set forth;

4. To differentiate on reasonable grounds between serious and minor offenses and to prescribe proportionate penalties for each;

5. To insure the public safety by preventing the commission of offenses through the deterrent influence of the sentences authorized; and

6. To impose just and deserved punishment on those whose conduct threatens the public peace; and

7. To promote truth and accountability in sentencing.

13-107. Time limitations

A. A prosecution for any homicide, misuse of public monies or a felony involving falsification of public records may be commenced at any time.

B. Except as otherwise provided in this section, prosecutions for other offenses must be commenced within the following periods after actual discovery by the state or the political subdivision having jurisdiction of the offense or discovery by the state or such political subdivision which should have occurred with the exercise of reasonable diligence, whichever first occurs:

1. For a class 2 through a class 6 felony, seven years.

2. For a misdemeanor, one year.

3. For a petty offense, six months.

C. For the purposes of subsection B, a prosecution is commenced when an indictment, information or complaint is filed.

D. The period of limitation does not run during any time when the accused is absent from the state or has no reasonably ascertainable place of abode within the state.

E. The time limitation within which a prosecution of a class 6 felony shall commence shall be determined pursuant to subsection B, paragraph 1, irrespective of whether a court enters a judgment of conviction for or a prosecuting attorney designates such offense as a misdemeanor.

F. If a complaint, indictment or information filed before the period of limitation has expired is dismissed for any reason, a new prosecution may be commenced within six months after the dismissal becomes final even if the period of limitation has expired at the time of the dismissal or will expire within six months of such dismissal.

CHAPTER 4 • JUSTIFICATION

13-401. Unavailability of justification defense; justification as defense

A. Even though a person is justified under this chapter in threatening or using physical force or deadly physical force against another, if in doing so such person recklessly injures or kills an innocent third person, the justification afforded by this chapter is unavailable in a prosecution for the reckless injury or killing of the innocent third person.

B. Except as provided in subsection A, justification as defined in this chapter is a defense in any prosecution for an offense pursuant to this title.

13-402. Justification; execution of public duty

A. Unless inconsistent with the other sections of this chapter defining justifiable use of physical force or deadly physical force or with some other superseding provision of law, conduct which would otherwise constitute an offense is justifiable when it is required or authorized by law.

B. The justification afforded by subsection A also applies if:

1. A reasonable person would believe such conduct is required or authorized by the judgment or direction of a competent court or tribunal or in the lawful execution of legal process, notwithstanding lack of jurisdiction of the court or defect in the legal process; or

2. A reasonable person would believe such conduct is required or authorized to assist a peace officer in the performance of such officer's duties, notwithstanding that the officer exceeded the officer's legal authority.

13-403. Justification; use of physical force

The use of physical force upon another person which would otherwise constitute an offense is justifiable and not criminal under any of the following circumstances:

1. A parent or guardian and a teacher or other person entrusted with the care and supervision of a minor or incompetent person may use reasonable and appropriate physical force upon the minor or incompetent person when and to the extent reasonably necessary and appropriate to maintain discipline.

2. A superintendent or other entrusted official of a jail, prison or correctional institution may use physical force for the preservation of peace to maintain order or discipline, or to prevent the commission of any felony or misdemeanor.

3. A person responsible for the maintenance of order in a place where others are assembled or on a common motor carrier of passengers or a person acting under his direction, may use physical force if and to the extent that a reasonable person would believe it necessary to maintain order, but such person may use deadly physical force only if reasonably necessary to prevent death or serious physical injury.

4. A person acting under a reasonable belief that another person is about to commit suicide or to inflict serious physical injury upon himself may use physical force upon that person to the extent reasonably necessary to thwart the result.

5. A duly licensed physician or a registered nurse or a person acting under his direction, or any other person who renders emergency care at the scene of an emergency occurrence, may use reasonable physical force for the purpose of administering a recognized and lawful form of treatment which is reasonably adapted to promoting the physical or mental health of the patient if:

(a) The treatment is administered with the consent of the patient or, if the patient is a minor or an incompetent person, with the consent of his parent, guardian or other person entrusted with his care and supervision except as otherwise provided by law; or

(b) The treatment is administered in an emergency when the person administering such treatment reasonably believes that no one competent to consent can be consulted and that a reasonable person, wishing to safeguard the welfare of the patient, would consent.

6. A person may otherwise use physical force upon another person as further provided in this chapter.

13-404. Justification; self-defense

A. Except as provided in subsection B of this section, a person is justified in threatening or using physical force against another when and to the extent a reasonable person would believe that physical force is immediately necessary to protect himself against the other's use or attempted use of unlawful physical force.

B. The threat or use of physical force against another is not justified:

1. In response to verbal provocation alone; or

2. To resist an arrest that the person knows or should know is being made by a peace officer or by a person acting in a peace officer's presence and at his direction, whether the arrest is lawful or unlawful, unless the physical force used by the peace officer exceeds that allowed by law; or

3. If the person provoked the other's use or attempted use of unlawful physical force, unless:

(a) The person withdraws from the encounter or clearly communicates to the other his intent to do so reasonably believing he cannot safely withdraw from the encounter; and

(b) The other nevertheless continues or attempts to use unlawful physical force against the person.

13-405. Justification; use of deadly physical force

A person is justified in threatening or using deadly physical force against another:

1. If such person would be justified in threatening or using physical force against the other under §13-404, and

2. When and to the degree a reasonable person would believe that deadly physical force is immediately necessary to protect himself against the other's use or attempted use of unlawful deadly physical force.

13-406. Justification; defense of a third person

A person is justified in threatening or using physical force or deadly physical force against another to protect a third person if:

1. Under the circumstances as a reasonable person would believe them to be, such person would be justified under §13-404 or 13-405 in threatening or using physical force or deadly physical force to protect himself against the unlawful physical force or deadly physical force a reasonable person would believe is threatening the third person he seeks to protect; and

2. A reasonable person would believe that such person's intervention is immediately necessary to protect the third person.

13-407. Justification; use of physical force in defense of premises

A. A person or his agent in lawful possession or control of premises is justified in threatening to use deadly physical force or in threatening or using physical force against another when and to the extent that a reasonable person would believe it immediately necessary to prevent or terminate the commission or attempted commission of a criminal trespass by the other person in or upon the premises.

B. A person may use deadly physical force under subsection A only in the defense of himself or third persons as described in sections 13-405 and 13-406.

C. In this section, "premises" means any real property and any structure, movable or immovable, permanent or temporary, adapted for both human residence and lodging whether occupied or not.

13-408. Justification; use of physical force in defense of property

A person is justified in using physical force against another when and to the extent that a reasonable person would believe it necessary to prevent what a reasonable person would believe is an attempt or commission by the other person of theft or criminal damage involving tangible movable property under his possession or control, but such person may use deadly physical force under these circumstances as provided in sections 13-405, 13-406 and 13-411.

13-409. Justification; use of physical force in law enforcement

A person is justified in threatening or using physical force against another if in making or assisting in making an arrest or detention or in preventing or assisting in preventing the escape after arrest or detention of that other person, such person uses or threatens to use physical force and all of the following exist:

1. A reasonable person would believe that such force is immediately necessary to effect the arrest or detention or prevent the escape.

2. Such person makes known the purpose of the arrest or detention or believes that it is otherwise known or cannot reasonably be made known to the person to be arrested or detained.

3. A reasonable person would believe the arrest or detention to be lawful.

13-410. Justification; use of deadly physical force in law enforcement

A. The threatened use of deadly physical force by a person against another is justified pursuant to §13-409 only if a reasonable person effecting the arrest or preventing the escape would believe the suspect or escapee is:

1. Actually resisting the discharge of a legal duty with deadly physical force or with the apparent capacity to use deadly physical force; or

2. A felon who has escaped from lawful confinement; or

3. A felon who is fleeing from justice or resisting arrest with physical force.

B. The use of deadly physical force by a person other than a peace officer against another is justified pursuant to §13-409 only if a reasonable person effecting the arrest or preventing the escape would believe the suspect or escapee is actually resisting the discharge of a legal duty with physical force or with the apparent capacity to use deadly physical force.

C. The use of deadly force by a peace officer against another is justified pursuant to §13-409 only when the peace officer reasonably believes that it is necessary:

1. To defend himself or a third person from what the peace officer reasonably believes to be the use or imminent use of deadly physical force.

2. To effect an arrest or prevent the escape from custody of a person whom the peace officer reasonably believes:

(a) Has committed, attempted to commit, is committing or is attempting to commit a felony involving the use or a threatened use of a deadly weapon.

(b) Is attempting to escape by use of a deadly weapon.

(c) Through past or present conduct of the person which is known by the peace officer that person is likely to endanger human life or inflict serious bodily injury to another unless apprehended without delay.

(d) Is necessary to lawfully suppress a riot if the person or another person participating in the riot is armed with a deadly weapon.

D. Not withstanding any other provisions of this chapter a peace officer is justified in threatening to use deadly physical force when and to the extent a reasonable officer believes it necessary to protect himself against another's potential use of physical force or deadly physical force.

13-411. Justification; use of force in crime prevention

A. A person is justified in threatening or using both physical force and deadly physical force against another if and to the extent the person reasonably believes that physical force or deadly physical force is immediately necessary to prevent the other's commission of arson of an occupied structure under §13-1704, burglary in the second or first degree under §13-1507 or 13-1508, kidnapping under §13-1304, manslaughter under §13-1103, second or first degree murder under §13-1104 or 13-1105, sexual conduct with a minor under §13-1405, sexual assault under §13-1406, child molestation under §13-1410, armed robbery under §13-1904, or aggravated assault under §13-1204, subsection A, paragraphs 1 and 2.

B. There is no duty to retreat before threatening or using deadly physical force justified by subsection A of this section.

C. A person is presumed to be acting reasonably for the purposes of this section if he is acting to prevent the commission of any of the offenses listed in subsection A of this section.

13-412. Duress

A. Conduct which would otherwise constitute an offense is justified if a reasonable person would believe that he was compelled to engage in the proscribed conduct by the threat or use of immediate physical force against his person or the person of another which resulted or could result in serious physical injury which a reasonable person in the situation would not have resisted.

B. The defense provided by subsection A is unavailable if the person intentionally, knowingly or recklessly placed himself in a situation in which it was probable that he would be subjected to duress.

C. The defense provided by subsection A is unavailable for offenses involving homicide or serious physical injury.

13-413. No civil liability for justified conduct

No person in this state shall be subject to civil liability for engaging in conduct otherwise justified pursuant to the provisions of this chapter.

13-415. Justification; domestic violence

If there have been past acts of domestic violence as defined in §13-3601, subsection A against the defendant by the victim, the state of mind of a reasonable person under sections 13-404, 13-405 and 13-406 shall be determined from the perspective of a reasonable person who has been a victim of those past acts of domestic violence.

CHAPTER 5 • RESPONSIBILITY

13-501. Immaturity
A person less than fourteen years old at the time of the conduct charged is not criminally responsible in the absence of clear proof that at the time of committing the conduct charged the person knew it was wrong.

CHAPTER 6 • CLASSIFICATIONS OF OFFENSES AND AUTHORIZED DISPOSITIONS OF OFFENDERS

13-601. Classification of offenses
A. Felonies are classified, for the purpose of sentence, into the following six categories:
1. Class 1 felonies.
2. Class 2 felonies.
3. Class 3 felonies.
4. Class 4 felonies.
5. Class 5 felonies.
6. Class 6 felonies.
B. Misdemeanors are classified, for the purpose of sentence, into the following three categories:
1. Class 1 misdemeanors.
2. Class 2 misdemeanors.
3. Class 3 misdemeanors.
C. Petty offenses are not classified.

13-602. Designation of offenses
A. The particular classification of each felony defined in this title is expressly designated in the section or chapter defining it. Any offense defined outside this title which is declared by law to be a felony without either specification of the classification or of the penalty is a class 5 felony.

B. The particular classification of each misdemeanor defined in this title is expressly designated in the section or chapter defining it. Any offense defined outside this title which is declared by law to be a misdemeanor without either specification of the classification or of the penalty is a Class 2 misdemeanor.

C. Every petty offense in this title is expressly designated as such. Any offense defined outside this title without either designation as a felony or misdemeanor or specification of the classification or the penalty is a petty offense.

CHAPTER 7 • IMPRISONMENT

13-701. Sentence of imprisonment for felony; presentence report
A. A sentence of imprisonment for a felony shall be a definite term of years and the person sentenced, unless otherwise provided by law, shall be committed to the custody of the state department of corrections.

B. No prisoner may be transferred to the custody of the state department of corrections without a certified copy of the judgment and sentence, signed by the sentencing judge, and a copy of a recent presentence investigation report unless the court has waived preparation of the report.

C. Except as provided in §13-604 the term of imprisonment for a felony shall be determined as follows for a first offense:
1. For a class 2 felony, five years.
2. For a class 3 felony, three and one-half years.
3. For a class 4 felony, two and one-half years.
4. For a class 5 felony, one and one-half years.
5. For a class 6 felony, one years.

13-702. Sentencing
A. Sentences provided in §13-701 for a first conviction of a felony, except those felonies involving a discharge, use or threatening exhibition of a deadly weapon or dangerous instrument or the intentional or knowing infliction of serious physical injury upon another or if a specific sentence is otherwise provided, may be increased or reduced by the court within the ranges set by this subsection. Such reduction or increase shall be based on the aggravating and mitigating circumstances contained in subsections C and D of this section and shall be within the following ranges:

	Minimum	Maximum
1. For a class 2 felony	4 years	10 years
2. For a class 3 felony	2.5 years	7 years
3. For a class 4 felony	1.5 years	3 years
4. For a class 5 felony	9 mos.	2 years
5. For a class 6 felony	6 mos.	1.5 years

13-707. Sentence of imprisonment for misdemeanor

A. A sentence of imprisonment for a misdemeanor shall be for a definite term to be served other than a place within custody of the state department of corrections. The court shall fix the term of imprisonment within the following maximum limitations:

1. For a class 1 misdemeanor, six months.

2. For a class 2 misdemeanor, four months.

3. For a class 3 misdemeanor, thirty days.

B. The court may, pursuant to this section, direct that the person sentenced shall not be released on any basis until the sentence imposed by the court has been served.

CHAPTER 8 • RESTITUTION AND FINES

13-801. Fines for felonies

A. A sentence to pay a fine for a felony shall be a sentence to pay an amount fixed by the court not more than one hundred fifty thousand dollars.

B. A judgment that the defendant shall pay a fine, with or without the alternative of imprisonment, shall constitute a lien in like manner as a judgment for money rendered in a civil action.

C. This section does not apply to an enterprise.

13-802. Fines for misdemeanors

A. A sentence to pay a fine for a class 1 misdemeanor shall be a sentence to pay an amount, fixed by the court, not more than two thousand five hundred dollars.

B. A sentence to pay a fine for a class 2 misdemeanor shall be a sentence to pay an amount, fixed by the court, not more than seven hundred fifty dollars.

C. A sentence to pay a fine for a class 3 misdemeanor shall be a sentence to pay an amount, fixed by the court, not more than five hundred dollars.

D. A sentence to pay a fine for a petty offense shall be a sentence to pay an amount, fixed by the court, of not more than three hundred dollars .

E. A judgment that the defendant shall pay a fine, with or without the alternative of imprisonment, shall constitute a lien in like manner as a judgment for money rendered in a civil action.

F. This section does not apply to an enterprise.

13-803. Fines against enterprises

A. A sentence to pay a fine, imposed on an enterprise for an offense defined in this title or for an offense defined outside this title for which no special enterprise fine is specified, shall be a sentence to pay an amount, fixed by the court, of not more than:

1. For a felony, one million dollars.

2. For a class 1 misdemeanor, twenty thousand dollars.

3. For a class 2 misdemeanor, ten thousand dollars.

4. For a class 3 misdemeanor, two thousand dollars.

5. For a petty offense, one thousand dollars.

B. A judgment that the enterprise shall pay a fine shall constitute a lien in like manner as a judgment for money rendered in a civil action.

CHAPTER 9 • PROBATION & RESTORATION OF CIVIL RIGHTS

13-904. Suspension of civil rights and occupational disabilities
A. A conviction for a felony suspends the following civil rights of the person sentenced:

1. The right to vote.

2. The right to hold public office of trust or profit.

3. The right to serve as a juror.

4. During any period of imprisonment any other civil rights the suspension of which is reasonably necessary for the security of the institution in which the person sentenced is confined or for the reasonable protection of the public.

5. The right to possess a gun or firearm.

H. A person who is adjudicated delinquent under §8-241 does not have the right to carry or possess a gun or firearm.

(NOTE: Chapter 9 also contains the extensive details for restoring civil rights and other material not included here.)

CHAPTER 11 • HOMICIDE

13-1101. Definitions
In this chapter, unless the context otherwise requires:

1. "Premeditation" means that the defendant acts with either the intention or the knowledge that he will kill another human being, when such intention or knowledge precedes the killing by a length of time to permit reflection. An act is not done with premeditation if it is the instant effect of a sudden quarrel or heat of passion.

2. "Homicide" means first degree murder, second degree murder, manslaughter or negligent homicide.

3. "Person" means a human being.

4. "Adequate provocation" means conduct or circumstances sufficient to deprive a reasonable person of self-control.

13-1102. Negligent homicide; classification
A. A person commits negligent homicide if with criminal negligence such person causes the death of another person.

B. Negligent homicide is a class 4 felony.

13-1103. Manslaughter; classification
A. A person commits manslaughter by:

1. Recklessly causing the death of another person, or

2. Committing second degree murder as defined in §13-1104, subsection A upon a sudden quarrel or heat of passion resulting from adequate provocation by the victim; or

3. Intentionally aiding another to commit suicide; or

4. Committing second degree murder as defined in §13-1104, subsection A, paragraph 3, while being coerced to do so by the use or threatened immediate use of unlawful deadly physical force upon such person or a third person which a reasonable person in his situation would have been unable to resist; or

5. Knowingly or recklessly causing the death of an unborn child at any stage of its development by any physical injury to the mother of such child which would be murder if the death of the mother had occurred.

B. Manslaughter is a class 3 felony.

13-1104. Second degree murder; classification
A. A person commits second degree murder if without premeditation:

1. Such person intentionally causes the death of another person; or

2. Knowing that his conduct will cause death or serious physical injury, such person causes the death of another person; or

3. Under circumstances manifesting extreme indifference to human life, such person recklessly engages in conduct which creates a grave risk of death and thereby causes the death of another person.

B. Second degree murder is a class 1 felony and is punishable as provided by §13-604, subsection N, §13-604.01 if the victim is under fifteen years of age or §13-710.

13-1105. First degree murder; classification
A. A person commits first degree murder if:

1. Intending or knowing that his conduct will cause death, such person causes the death of another with premeditation; or

2. Acting either alone or with one or more other persons such person commits or attempts to commit

sexual conduct with a minor under §13-1405, sexual assault under §13-1406, molestation of a child under §13-1410, marijuana offenses under §13-3405, subsection A, paragraph 4, dangerous drug offenses under §13-3407, subsection A, paragraph 7, narcotics offenses under §13-3408, subsection A, paragraph 7 that equal or exceed the statutory threshold amount for each offense or combination of offenses, involving or using minors in drug offenses under §13-3409, kidnapping under §13-1304, burglary under §13-1506, 13-1507 or 13-1508, arson under §13-1704, robbery under §13-1902, 13-1903 or 13-1904, escape under §13-2503 or 13-2504, child abuse under §13-3623, subsection B, paragraph 1, or unlawful flight from a pursuing law enforcement vehicle under §28-622.01 and in the course of and in furtherance of such offense or immediate flight from such offense, such person or another person causes the death of any person.

B. Homicide, as defined in subsection A, paragraph 2 of this section, requires no specific mental state other than what is required for the commission of any of the enumerated felonies.

C. First degree murder is a class 1 felony and is punishable by death or life imprisonment as provided by §13-703.

CHAPTER 12 • ASSAULT AND RELATED OFFENSES

13-1201. Endangerment; classification

A. A person commits endangerment by recklessly endangering another person with a substantial risk of imminent death or physical injury.

B. Endangerment involving a substantial risk of imminent death is a class 6 felony. In all other cases, it is a class 1 misdemeanor.

13-1202. Threatening or intimidating; classification

A. A person commits threatening or intimidating if such person threatens or intimidates by word or conduct:

1. To cause physical injury to another person or serious damage to the property of another; or

2. To cause, or in reckless disregard to causing, serious public inconvenience including, but not limited to, evacuation of a building, place of assembly, or transportation facility; or

3. To cause physical injury to another person or damage to the property of another in order to promote, further or assist in the interests of or to cause, induce or solicit another person to participate in a criminal street gang, a criminal syndicate or a racketeering enterprise.

B. Threatening or intimidating pursuant to subsection A, paragraph 1 or 2 is a class 1 misdemeanor. Threatening or intimidating pursuant to subsection A, paragraph 3 is a class 4 felony.

13-1203. Assault; classification

A. A person commits assault by:

1. Intentionally, knowingly or recklessly causing any physical injury to another person; or

2. Intentionally placing another person in reasonable apprehension of imminent physical injury; or

3. Knowingly touching another person with the intent to injure, insult or provoke such person.

B. Assault committed intentionally or knowingly pursuant to subsection A, paragraph 1 is a class 1 misdemeanor. Assault committed recklessly pursuant to subsection A, paragraph 1 or assault pursuant to subsection A, paragraph 2 is a class 2 misdemeanor. Assault committed pursuant to subsection A, paragraph 3 is a class 3 misdemeanor.

13-1204. Aggravated assault; classification

A. A person commits aggravated assault if such person commits assault as defined in §13-1203 under any of the following circumstances:

1. If such person causes serious physical injury to another.

2. If such person uses a deadly weapon or dangerous instrument.

3. If such person commits the assault after entering the private home of another with the intent to commit the assault.

4. If such person is eighteen years of age or more and commits the assault upon a child the age of fifteen years or under.

5. If such person commits the assault knowing or having reason to know that the victim is a peace officer, or a person summoned and directed by such officer while engaged in the execution of any official duties.

6. If such person commits the assault knowing or having reason to know the victim is a teacher or other person employed by any school and such teacher or other employee is upon the grounds of a school or grounds adjacent to such school or is in any part of a building or vehicle used for school purposes, or any teacher or school nurse visiting a private home in the course of his professional duties, or any teacher engaged in any authorized and organized classroom activity held on other than school grounds.

7. If such person is imprisoned in the custody of the state department of corrections, a law enforcement agency, county or city jail, or adult or juvenile detention facility of a city or county or subject to the custody of personnel from such department, agency, jail or detention facility and commits the

assault knowing or having reason to know the victim is an employee of such department, agency, jail or detention facility acting in an official capacity.

8. If such person commits the assault while the victim is bound or otherwise physically restrained or while the victim's capacity to resist is substantially impaired.

9. If such person commits the assault knowing or having reason to know that the victim is a firefighter, fire investigator, fire inspector, emergency medical technician or paramedic engaged in the execution of any official duties, or a person summoned and directed by such individual while engaged in the execution of any official duties.

10. If such person commits the assault knowing or having reason to know that the victim is a licensed health care practitioner who is certified or licensed pursuant to title 32, chapters 13, 15, 17 or 25, or a person summoned and directed by such licensed health care practitioner while engaged in his professional duties. The provisions of this paragraph do not apply if the person who commits the assault is seriously mentally ill, as defined in §36-550 or to persons afflicted with Alzheimer's disease or related dementia.

11. If such person commits assault by any means of force which causes temporary but substantial disfigurement, temporary but substantial loss or impairment of any body organ or part, or a fracture of any body part.

B. Aggravated assault pursuant to subsection A, paragraph 1 or 2 of this section is a class 3 felony except if the victim is under fifteen years of age in which case it is a class 2 felony punishable pursuant to §13-604.01. Aggravated assault pursuant to subsection A, paragraph 11 of this section is a class 4 felony. Aggravated assault pursuant to subsection A, paragraph 7 of this section is a class 5 felony. Aggravated assault pursuant to subsection A, paragraph 3, 4, 5, 6, 8, 9 or 10 of this section is a class 6 felony.

13-1209. Drive by shootings; classification; definitions

A. A person commits drive by shooting by intentionally discharging a weapon from a motor vehicle at a person, another occupied motor vehicle or an occupied structure.

B. Drive by shooting is a class 2 felony.

C. As used in this section:

1. "Motor vehicle" has the same meaning as prescribed in §28-101.

2. "Occupied structure" has the same meaning as prescribed in §13-3101.

CHAPTER 13 • KIDNAPPING AND RELATED OFFENSES

13-1304. Kidnapping; classification; consecutive sentence

A. A person commits kidnapping by knowingly restraining another person with the intent to:

1. Hold the victim for ransom, as a shield or hostage; or

2. Hold the victim for involuntary servitude; or

3. Inflict death, physical injury or a sexual offense on the victim, or to otherwise aid in the commission of a felony; or

4. Place the victim or a third person in reasonable apprehension of imminent physical injury to the victim or such third person.

5. Interfere with the performance of a governmental or political function.

6. Seize or exercise control over any airplane, train, bus, ship or other vehicle.

B. Kidnapping is a class 2 felony unless the victim is released voluntarily by the defendant without physical injury in a safe place prior to arrest and prior to accomplishing any of the further enumerated offenses in subsection A of this section in which case it is a class 4 felony. If the victim is released pursuant to an agreement with the state and without any physical injury, it is a class 3 felony. If the victim is under fifteen years of age kidnapping is a class 2 felony punishable pursuant to §13-604.01. The sentence for kidnapping of a victim under fifteen years of age shall run consecutively to any other sentence imposed on the defendant and to any undischarged term of imprisonment of the defendant.

CHAPTER 14 • SEXUAL OFFENSES

13-1405. Sexual conduct with a minor; classifications

A. A person commits sexual conduct with a minor by intentionally or knowingly engaging in sexual intercourse or oral sexual contact with any person who is under eighteen years of age.

B. Sexual conduct with a minor under fifteen years of age is a class 2 felony and is punishable pursuant to §13-604.01. Sexual conduct with a minor fifteen years of age or over is a class 6 felony.

13-1406. Sexual assault; classifications

A. A person commits sexual assault by intentionally or knowingly engaging in sexual intercourse or oral sexual contact with any person without consent of such person.

B. Sexual assault is a class 2 felony, and the person convicted shall be sentenced pursuant to this section and the person is not eligible for suspension of sentence, probation, pardon or release from confinement on any basis except as specifically authorized by §31-233, subsection A or B until the sentence imposed by the court has been served or commuted. If the victim is under 15 years of age, sexual assault is punishable pursuant to §13-604.01. The presumptive term may be aggravated or mitigated within the range under this section pursuant to §13-702, subsections B, C and D. The term for a first offense is as follows:

Minimum	Presumptive	Maximum
5.25 years	7 years	14 years

13-1410. Molestation of child; classification
   A person commits molestation of a child by intentionally or knowingly engaging in or causing a person to engage in sexual contact, except sexual contact with the female breast, with a child under fifteen years of age.
   B. Molestation of a child is a class 2 felony that is punishable pursuant to §13-604.01.

CHAPTER 15 • CRIMINAL TRESPASS AND BURGLARY

13-1502. Criminal trespass in the third degree; classification
   A. A person commits criminal trespass in the third degree by:
   1. Knowingly entering or remaining unlawfully on any real property after a reasonable request to leave by the owner or any other person having lawful control over such property, or reasonable notice prohibiting entry.
   2. Knowingly entering or remaining unlawfully on the right-of-way for tracks, or the storage or switching yards or rolling stock of a railroad company.
   B. Criminal trespass in the third degree is a class 3 misdemeanor.

13-1503. Criminal trespass in the second degree; classification
   A. A person commits criminal trespass in the second degree by knowingly entering or remaining unlawfully in or on any nonresidential structure or in any fenced commercial yard.
   B. Criminal trespass in the second degree is a class 2 misdemeanor.

13-1504. Criminal trespass in the first degree; classification
   A. A person commits criminal trespass in the first degree by knowingly:
   1. Entering or remaining unlawfully in or on a residential structure or in a fenced residential yard; or
   2. Entering any residential yard and, without lawful authority, looking into the residential structure thereon in reckless disregard of infringing on the inhabitant's right of privacy.
   3. Entering unlawfully on real property subject to a valid mineral claim or lease with the intent to hold, work, take or explore for minerals on such claim or lease.
   4. Entering or remaining unlawfully on the property of another and burning, defacing, mutilating or otherwise desecrating a religious symbol or other religious property of another without the express permission of the owner of the property.
   B. Criminal trespass in the first degree is a class 6 felony if it is committed by entering or remaining unlawfully in or on a residential structure or committed pursuant to subsection A, paragraph 4. Criminal trespass in the first degree is a class 1 misdemeanor if it is committed by entering or remaining unlawfully in a fenced residential yard or committed pursuant to subsection A, paragraph 2 or 3.

13-1506. Burglary in the third degree; classification
   A. A person commits burglary in the third degree by entering or remaining unlawfully in or on a nonresidential structure or in a fenced commercial or residential yard with the intent to commit any theft or any felony therein.
   B. Burglary in the third degree is a class 4 felony.

13-1507. Burglary in the second degree; classification
   A. A person commits burglary in the second degree by entering or remaining unlawfully in or on a residential structure with the intent to commit any theft or any felony therein.
   B. Burglary in the second degree is a class 3 felony.

13- 1508 . Burglary in the first degree; classification
   A. A person commits burglary in the first degree if such person or an accomplice violates the provisions of either §13-1506 or 13-1507 and knowingly possesses explosives, a deadly weapon or a dangerous instrument in the course of committing any theft or any felony.
   B. Burglary in the first degree of a nonresidential structure or a fenced commercial or residential yard is a class 3 felony. It is a class 2 felony if committed in a residential structure.

CHAPTER 17 • ARSON

13-1704. Arson of an occupied structure; classification
A. A person commits arson of an occupied structure by knowingly and unlawfully damaging an occupied structure by knowingly causing a fire or explosion.
B. Arson of an occupied structure is a class 2 felony.

CHAPTER 19 • ROBBERY

13-1902. Robbery; classification
A. A person commits robbery if in the course of taking any property of another from his person or immediate presence and against his will, such person threatens or uses force against any person with intent either to coerce surrender of property or to prevent resistance to such person taking or retaining property.
B. Robbery is a class 4 felony.

13-1903. Aggravated robbery; classification
A. A person commits aggravated robbery if in the course of committing robbery as defined in §13-1902 such person is aided by one or more accomplices actually present.
B. Aggravated robbery is a class 3 felony.

13-1904. Armed robbery; classification
A. A person commits armed robbery if, in the course of committing robbery as defined in §13-1902, such person or an accomplice:
1. Is armed with a deadly weapon or a simulated deadly weapon; or
2. Uses or threatens to use a deadly weapon or dangerous instrument or a simulated deadly weapon.
B. Armed robbery is a class 2 felony.

CHAPTER 24 • OBSTRUCTION OF PUBLIC ADMINISTRATION

13-2403. Refusing to aid a peace officer; classification
A. A person commits refusing to aid a peace officer if, upon a reasonable command by a person reasonably known to be a peace officer such person knowingly refuses or fails to aid such peace officer in:
1. Effectuating or securing an arrest; or
2. Preventing the commission by another of any offense.
B. A person who complies with this section by aiding a peace officer shall not be held liable to any person for damages resulting therefrom, provided such person acted reasonably under the circumstances known to him at the time.
C. Refusing to aid a peace officer is a class 1 misdemeanor.

13-2409. Obstructing criminal investigations or prosecutions; classification
A person who knowingly attempts by means of bribery, misrepresentation, intimidation or force or threats of force to obstruct, delay or prevent the communication of information or testimony relating to a violation of any criminal statute to a peace officer, magistrate, prosecutor or grand jury or who knowingly injures another in his person or property on account of the giving by the latter or by any other person of any such information or testimony to a peace officer, magistrate, prosecutor or grand jury is guilty of a class 5 felony.

CHAPTER 25 • ESCAPE AND RELATED OFFENSES

13 2502. Escape in the third degree; classification
A. A person commits escape in the third degree if, having been arrested for, charged with or found guilty of a misdemeanor or petty offense, such person knowingly escapes or attempts to escape from custody.
B. Escape in the third degree is a class 6 felony.

13-2503. Escape in the second degree; classification

A. A person commits escape in the second degree by knowingly:

1. Escaping or attempting to escape from a correctional facility; or

2. Escaping or attempting to escape from custody imposed as a result of having been arrested for, charged with or found guilty of a felony.

B. Escape in the second degree is a class 5 felony and the sentence imposed for a violation of this section shall run consecutively to any sentence of imprisonment for which the defendant was confined or to any term of conditional release from the sentence including probation, parole, work furlough or any other release.

13-2504. Escape in the first degree; classification

A. A person commits escape in the first degree by knowingly escaping or attempting to escape from custody or a correctional facility by:

1. Using or threatening the use of physical force against another person; or

2. Using or threatening to use a deadly weapon or dangerous instrument against another person.

B. Escape in the first degree is a class 4 felony and the sentence imposed for a violation of this section shall run consecutively to any sentence of imprisonment for which the defendant was confined or to any term of conditional release from the sentence including probation, parole, work furlough or any other release.

13-2505. Promoting prison contraband; classification; exceptions; x-radiation

A. A person, not otherwise authorized by law, commits promoting prison contraband:

1. By knowingly taking contraband into a correctional facility or the grounds of such facility; or

2. By knowingly conveying contraband to any person confined in a correctional facility; or

3. By knowingly making, obtaining or possessing contraband while being confined in a correctional facility or while being lawfully transported or moved incident to correctional facility confinement.

B. Any person who has reasonable grounds to believe there has been a violation or attempted violation of this section shall immediately report such violation or attempted violation to the official in charge of the facility or to a peace officer.

C. Promoting prison contraband if the contraband is a deadly weapon, dangerous instrument or explosive is a class 2 felony. Promoting prison contraband if the contraband is a dangerous drug, narcotic drug or marijuana is a class 2 felony. In all other cases promoting prison contraband is a class 5 felony. Failure to report a violation or attempted violation of this section is a class 5 felony.

13-2508. Resisting arrest; classification

A. A person commits resisting arrest by intentionally preventing or attempting to prevent a person reasonably known to him to be a peace officer, acting under color of such peace officer's official authority, from effecting an arrest by:

1. Using or threatening to use physical force against the peace officer or another; or

2. Using any other means creating a substantial risk of causing physical injury to the peace officer or another.

B. Resisting arrest is a class 6 felony.

13-2510. Hindering prosecution; definition

For purposes of §13-2511 and §13-2512 a person renders assistance to another person by knowingly:

1. Harboring or concealing the other person; or

2. Warning the other person of impending discovery, apprehension prosecution or conviction. This does not apply to a warning given in connection with an effort to bring another into compliance with the law; or

3. Providing the other person with money, transportation, a weapon, a disguise or other similar means of avoiding discovery, apprehension, prosecution or conviction; or

4. Preventing or obstructing by means of force, deception or intimidation anyone from performing an act that might aid in the discovery, apprehension, prosecution or conviction of the other person; or

5. Suppressing by an act of concealment, alteration or destruction any physical evidence that might aid in the discovery, apprehension, prosecution or conviction of the other person; or

6. Concealing the identity of the other person.

13-2511. Hindering prosecution in the second degree; classification

A. A person commits hindering prosecution in the second degree if, with the intent to hinder the apprehension, prosecution, conviction or punishment of another for any misdemeanor or petty offense, such person renders assistance to such person.

B. Hindering prosecution in the second degree is a class 1 misdemeanor.

13-2512. Hindering prosecution in the first degree; classification

A. A person commits hindering prosecution in the first degree if with the intent to hinder the apprehension, prosecution, conviction or punishment of another for any felony, such person renders assistance to such person.

B. Hindering prosecution in the first degree is a class 5 felony.

CHAPTER 27 • PERJURY AND RELATED OFFENSES

13-2702. Perjury; classification

A. A person commits perjury by making a false sworn statement in regard to a material issue, believing it to be false.

B. Perjury is a class 4 felony.

CHAPTER 28 • INTERFERENCE WITH JUDICIAL AND OTHER PROCEEDINGS

13-2809. Tampering with physical evidence; classification

A. A person commits tampering with physical evidence if, with intent that it be used, introduced, rejected or unavailable in an official proceeding which is then pending or which such person knows is about to be instituted, such person:

1. Destroys, mutilates, alters, conceals or removes physical evidence with the intent to impair its verity or availability; or

2. Knowingly makes, produces or offers any false physical evidence; or

3. Prevents the production of physical evidence by an act of force, intimidation or deception against any person.

B. Inadmissibility of the evidence in question is not a defense.

C. Tampering with physical evidence is a class 6 felony.

CHAPTER 29 • OFFENSES AGAINST PUBLIC ORDER

13-2904. Disorderly conduct; classification

A. A person commits disorderly conduct if, with intent to disturb the peace or quiet of a neighborhood, family or person, or with knowledge of doing so, such person:

1. Engages in fighting, violent or seriously disruptive behavior; or

2 Makes unreasonable noise; or

3. Uses abusive or offensive language or gestures to any person present in a manner likely to provoke immediate physical retaliation by such person; or

4. Makes any protracted commotion, utterance or display with the intent to prevent the transaction of the business of a lawful meeting, gathering or procession; or

5. Refuses to obey a lawful order to disperse issued to maintain public safety in dangerous proximity to a fire, a hazard or any other emergency; or

6. Recklessly handles, displays or discharges a deadly weapon or dangerous instrument.

B. Disorderly conduct under subsection A, paragraph 6 is a class 6 felony. Disorderly conduct under subsection A, paragraph 1, 2, 3, 4 or 5 is a class 1 misdemeanor.

13-2908. Criminal nuisance; classification

A. A person commits criminal nuisance:

1. If, by conduct either unlawful in itself or unreasonable under the circumstances, such person recklessly creates or maintains a condition which endangers the safety or health of others.

2. By knowingly conducting or maintaining any premises, place or resort where persons gather for purposes of engaging in unlawful conduct.

Criminal nuisance is a class 3 misdemeanor.

13-2911. Interference with the peaceful conduct of educational institutions; definitions; violation; classification

A. A person commits interference with the peaceful conduct of educational institutions by knowingly:

1. Going upon or remaining upon the property of any educational institution in violation of any rule of such institution or for the purpose of interfering with the lawful use of such property by others or in such manner as to deny or interfere with the lawful use of such property by others; or

2. Refusing to obey a lawful order given pursuant to subsection B of this section.

B. When the chief administrative officer of an educational institution or an officer or employee designated by him to maintain order has reasonable grounds to believe that any person or persons are committing any act which interferes with or disrupts the lawful use of such property by others at the educational institution or has reasonable grounds to believe any person has entered upon the property for the purpose of committing such an act, such officer or employee may order such person to leave the property of the educational institution.

C. The appropriate governing board of every educational institution shall adopt rules for the maintenance of public order upon all property under its jurisdiction which is used for educational purposes and shall provide a program for the enforcement of such rules. Such rules shall govern the conduct of students, faculty and other staff and all members of the public while on the property. Penalties for violations of such rules shall be clearly set forth and enforced. Penalties shall include provisions for the ejection of a violator from the property and, in the case of a student, faculty member or other staff violator, his suspension, expulsion or other appropriate disciplinary action. Adoption of all rules required by this section shall be governed by title 41, chapter 6, and such rules shall be amended as necessary to ensure the maintenance of public order. Any deadly weapon, dangerous instrument or explosive used, displayed or possessed by a person in violation of a rule adopted pursuant to this subsection shall be forfeited and sold, destroyed, or otherwise disposed of according to chapter 39 of this title. Nothing in this subsection shall preclude school districts from conducting approved gun safety programs on school campuses. This subsection shall not apply to private universities, colleges, high schools or common schools or other private educational institutions.

H. Interference with the peaceful conduct of educational institutions is a class 1 misdemeanor.

CHAPTER 31 • WEAPONS AND EXPLOSIVES

13-3101. Definitions
In this chapter, unless the context otherwise requires:

1. "Deadly weapon" means anything designed for lethal use. The term includes a firearm.

2. "Deface" means to remove, alter or destroy the manufacturer's serial number.

3. "Explosive" means any dynamite, nitroglycerine, black powder or other similar explosive material including plastic explosives but does not mean or include ammunition or ammunition components such as primers, percussion caps, smokeless powder, black powder and black powder substitutes used for hand loading purposes.

4. "Firearm" means any loaded or unloaded pistol, revolver, rifle, shotgun or other weapon which will or is designed to or may readily be converted to expel a projectile by the action of an explosive, except that it does not include a firearm in permanently inoperable condition.

5. "Occupied structure" means any building, object, vehicle, watercraft, aircraft or place with sides and a floor, separately securable from any other structure attached to it and used for lodging, business, transportation, recreation or storage in which one or more human beings either is or is likely to be present or so near as to be in equivalent danger at the time the discharge of a firearm occurs. The term includes any dwelling house, whether occupied, unoccupied or vacant.

6. "Prohibited possessor" means any person:

(a) Who has been found to constitute a danger to himself or to others pursuant to court order under the provisions of §36-540, and whose court ordered treatment has not been terminated by court order.

(b) Who has been convicted within or without this state of a felony or who has been adjudicated delinquent and whose civil right to possess or carry a gun or firearm has not been restored.

(c) Who is at the time of possession serving a term of imprisonment in any correctional or detention facility.

(d) Who is at the time of possession serving a term of probation, parole, community supervision, work furlough, home arrest or release on any other basis or who is serving a term of probation or parole pursuant to the interstate compact under title 31, chapter 3, article 4.

7. "Prohibited weapon" means, but does not include, fireworks imported, distributed or used in compliance with state laws or local ordinances, any propellant, propellant actuated devices or propellant actuated industrial tools which are manufactured, imported or distributed for their intended purposes or a device which is commercially manufactured primarily for the purpose of illumination, any:

(a) Explosive, incendiary or poison gas:

(i) Bomb.

(ii) Grenade.

(iii) Rocket having a propellant charge of more than four ounces.

(iv) Mine; or

(b) Device designed, made or adapted to muffle the report of a firearm; or

(c) Firearm that is capable of shooting more than one shot automatically, without manual reloading, by a single function of the trigger; or

(d) Rifle with a barrel length of less than sixteen inches, or shotgun with a barrel length of less than eighteen inches, or any firearm made from a rifle or shotgun which, as modified, has an overall length of less than twenty-six inches; or

(e) Instrument, including a nunchaku, that consists of two or more sticks, clubs, bars or rods to be used as handles, connected by a rope, cord, wire or chain, in the design of a weapon used in connection with the practice of a system of self-defense; or

(f) Breakable container which contains a flammable liquid with a flash point of one hundred fifty degrees Fahrenheit or less and has a wick or similar device capable of being ignited; or

(g) Combination of parts or materials designed and intended for use in making or converting a device into an item set forth in subdivision (a) or (f) of this paragraph. The items as set forth in subdivisions (a), (b), (c) and (d) of this paragraph shall not include any such firearms or devices registered in the national firearms registry and transfer records of the United States treasury department or any firearm which has been classified as a curio or relic by the United States treasury department.

13-3102. Misconduct involving weapons, defenses, classification, definitions
    A. A person commits misconduct involving weapons by knowingly:
    1. Carrying a deadly weapon without a permit pursuant to §13-3112 except a pocket knife concealed on his person; or
    2. Carrying a deadly weapon without a permit pursuant to §13-3112 concealed within immediate control of any person in or on a means of transportation; or
    3. Manufacturing, possessing, transporting, selling or transferring a prohibited weapon; or
    4. Possessing a deadly weapon if such person is a prohibited possessor; or
    5. Selling or transferring a deadly weapon to a prohibited possessor; or
    6. Defacing a deadly weapon; or
    7. Possessing a defaced deadly weapon knowing the deadly weapon was defaced; or
    8. Using or possessing a deadly weapon during the commission of any felony offense included in chapter 34 of this title; or
    9. Discharging a firearm at an occupied structure in order to assist, promote or further the interests of a criminal street gang, a criminal syndicate or a racketeering enterprise; or
    10. Unless specifically authorized by law, entering any public establishment or attending any public event and carrying a deadly weapon on his person after a reasonable request by the operator of the establishment or the sponsor of the event or his agent to remove his weapon and place it in the custody of the operator of the establishment or the sponsor of the event; or
    11. Unless specifically authorized by law, entering an election polling place on the day of any election carrying a deadly weapon; or
    12. Possessing a deadly weapon on school grounds; or
    13. Unless specifically authorized by law, entering a commercial nuclear generating station carrying a deadly weapon on his person or within the immediate control of any person.
    B. A person commits misconduct involving weapons by supplying, selling or giving possession or control of a firearm to another person if the person knows or has reason to know that the other person would use the firearm in the commission of any felony.
    C. Subsection A, paragraph 1 of this section shall not apply to a person in his dwelling, on his business premises or on real property owned or leased by that person.
    D. Subsection A, paragraphs 1, 2, 3, 7, 10, 11, 12 and 13 of this section shall not apply to:
    1. A peace officer or any person summoned by any peace officer to assist and while actually assisting in the performance of official duties; or
    2. A member of the military forces of the United States or of any state of the United States in the performance of official duties; or
    3. A person specifically licensed, authorized or permitted pursuant to a statute of this state or of the United States.
    E. Subsection A, paragraphs 3 and 7 of this section shall not apply to:
    1. The possessing, transporting, selling or transferring of weapons by a museum as a part of its collection or an educational institution for educational purposes or by an authorized employee of such museum or institution, if:
    (a) Such museum or institution is operated by the United States or this state or a political subdivision of this state, or by an organization described in §170(c) of title 26 of the United States Code as a recipient of a charitable contribution; and
    (b) Reasonable precautions are taken with respect to theft or misuse of such material.
    2. The regular and lawful transporting as merchandise; or
    3. Acquisition by a person by operation of law such as by gift, devise or descent or in a fiduciary capacity as a recipient of the property or former property of an insolvent, incapacitated or deceased person.
    F. Subsection A, paragraph 3 of this section shall not apply to the merchandise of an authorized manufacturer thereof or dealer therein, when such material is intended to be manufactured, possessed, transported, sold or transferred solely for or to a dealer or a regularly constituted or appointed state, county or municipal police department or police officer, or a detention facility, or the military service of this or another state or the United States, or a museum or educational institution or a person specifically licensed or permitted pursuant to federal or state law.
    G. Subsection A, paragraph 1 of this section shall not apply to a weapon or weapons carried in a belt holster which holster is wholly or partially visible, or carried in a scabbard or case designed for carrying weapons which scabbard or case is wholly or partially visible or carried in luggage. Subsection A, paragraph 2 of this section shall not apply to a weapon or weapons carried in a case, holster, scabbard, pack or luggage which is carried within a means of transportation or within a storage compartment, trunk or glove compartment of a means of transportation.
    H. Subsection A, paragraph 10 of this section shall not apply to shooting ranges or shooting events, hunting areas or similar locations or activities.
    I. Subsection A, paragraph 3 of this section shall not apply to a weapon described in §13-3101, paragraph 7, subdivision (e), if such weapon is possessed for the purposes of preparing for, conducting

or participating in lawful exhibitions, demonstrations, contests or athletic events involving the use of such weapon. Subsection A, paragraph 12 of this section shall not apply to a weapon if such weapon is possessed for the purposes of preparing for, conducting or participating in hunter or firearm safety courses.

J. Subsection A, paragraph 12 of this section shall not apply to the possession of a:

1. Firearm which is not loaded and which is carried within a means of transportation under the control of an adult provided that if the adult leaves the means of transportation the firearm shall not be visible from the outside of the means of transportation and the means of transportation shall be locked.

2. Firearm for use on the school grounds in a program approved by a school.

K. Misconduct involving weapons under subsection A, paragraph 9 or subsection B of this section is a class 3 felony. Misconduct involving weapons under subsection A, paragraph 3, 4 or 8 of this section is a class 4 felony. Misconduct involving weapons under subsection A, paragraph 12 of this section is a class 1 misdemeanor unless the violation occurs in connection with conduct which violates the provisions of §13-2308, subsection A, paragraph 5, §13-2312, subsection C, §13-3409 or §13-3411, in which case the offense is a class 6 felony. Misconduct involving weapons under subsection A, paragraphs 5, 6 and 7 of this section is a class 6 felony. Misconduct involving weapons under subsection A, paragraphs 1, 2, 10, 11 and 13 of this section is a class 1 misdemeanor.

L. For purposes of this section:

1. "School" means a public or nonpublic kindergarten program, common school or high school.

2. "School grounds" means in, or on the grounds of, a school.

13-3103. Misconduct involving explosives; classification

A. A person commits misconduct involving explosives by knowingly:

1. Keeping or storing a greater quantity than fifty pounds of explosives in or upon any building or premises within a distance of one-half mile of the exterior limits of a city or town, except in vessels, railroad cars or vehicles receiving and keeping them in the course of and for the purpose of transportation; or

2. Keeping or storing percussion caps or any blasting powder within two hundred feet of a building or premises where explosives are kept or stored; or

3. Selling, transporting or possessing explosives without having plainly marked, in a conspicuous place on the box or package containing the explosive, its name, explosive character and date of manufacture.

4. This section shall not apply to any person who legally keeps, stores or transports explosives, percussion caps or blasting powder as a part of their business.

B. Misconduct involving explosives is a class 1 misdemeanor.

13-3104. Depositing explosives; classification

A. A person commits depositing explosives if with the intent to physically endanger, injure, intimidate or terrify any person, such person knowingly deposits any explosive on, in or near any vehicle, building or place where persons inhabit, frequent or assemble.

B. Depositing explosives is a class 4 felony.

13-3105. Forfeiture of weapons and explosives

A. Upon the conviction of any person for the violation of any felony in this state in which a deadly weapon, dangerous instrument or explosive was used, displayed or unlawfully possessed by such person the court shall order the article forfeited and sold, destroyed or otherwise properly disposed.

B. Upon the conviction of any person for the violation of §13-2904, subsection A, paragraph 6 or §13-3102, subsection A, paragraph 1, 2, 8 or 10, the court may order the forfeiture of the deadly weapon or dangerous instrument involved in the offense.

C. If at any time the court finds pursuant to rule 11 of the Arizona rules of criminal procedure that a person who is charged with a violation of this title is incompetent, the court shall order that any deadly weapon, dangerous instrument or explosive used, displayed or unlawfully possessed by the person during the commission of the alleged offense be forfeited and sold, destroyed or otherwise properly disposed.

13-3106. Firearm purchase in other states

A person residing in this state, or a corporation or other business entity maintaining a place of business in this state, may purchase or otherwise obtain firearms anywhere in the United States if such purchase or acquisition fully complies with the laws of this state and the state in which the purchase or acquisition is made and the purchaser and seller, prior to the sale or delivery for sale, have complied with all the requirements of the federal gun control act of 1968, public law 90-618, §922, subsection (c) and the code of federal regulations, volume 26, §178.96, subsection (c).

13-3107. Control of firearms, hunting and rifle ranges within municipalities; classification

A. Discharge of a firearm within the limits of any municipality is a class 2 misdemeanor except:

1. As allowed pursuant to the provisions of chapter 4 of this title.

2. On a properly supervised range.

3. In an area recommended as a hunting area by the Arizona game and fish department, approved and posted as required by the chief of police, but any such area may be closed when deemed unsafe by the chief of police or the director of the game and fish department.

4. For the control of nuisance wildlife by permit from the Arizona game and fish department or the United States fish and wildlife service.

5. By special permit of the chief of police of the municipality.

6. As required by an animal control officer in the performance of duties as specified in §9-499.04.

B. A properly supervised range for the purposes of this section means a range operated by a club affiliated with the national rifle association of America, the amateur trapshooting association, the national skeet association, or any other nationally recognized shooting organization, any agency of the federal government, state of Arizona, county or city within which the range is located, or any public or private school, and, in the case of air or carbon dioxide gas operated guns, or underground ranges on private or public property, such ranges may be operated with adult supervision.

13-3108. Firearms regulated by state; state preemption

A. Ordinances of any political subdivision of this state relating to the transportation, possession, carrying, sale and use of firearms in this state shall not be in conflict with this chapter.

B. A political subdivision of this state shall not require the licensing or registration of firearms or prohibit the ownership, purchase, sale or transfer of firearms.

13-3108.01. Handgun clearance center

A. By October 1, 1994 the department of public safety shall establish an instant background check system to determine whether purchases, sales or transfers of handguns to any person violate any federal law or any law of this state prohibiting the possession of handguns.

B. The instant background check system shall be known as the Arizona handgun clearance center. The handgun clearance center shall establish procedures for providing information to licensed firearms dealers regarding whether a purchaser or transferee is a felon, a fugitive from justice or is disqualified from lawfully possessing a handgun by any federal law or law of this state.

C. The handgun clearance center may promulgate rules establishing an appeals process to allow any person denied the sale or transfer of a handgun to determine the basis for the denial of any sale or transfer of a handgun based on information provided by the handgun clearance center. The only relief to which the person is entitled is the correction of information reasonably relied upon by the handgun clearance center.

D. To the extent permitted by federal law or the laws of this state governing criminal history records information, the director of the department of public safety may establish a procedure for contracting with private sector enterprises to conduct instant background checks.

E. This section does not apply to private handgun sales or transfers which are not subject to any federal law or any other law of this state.

Conditional repeal

If the Brady Handgun Violence Protection *(sic)* Act (P.L. 103-159) is repealed or if there is a final determination by a court of competent jurisdiction that the Brady Handgun Violence Protection *(sic)* Act is unconstitutional, §13-3108.01, Arizona Revised Statutes, is repealed.
(NOTE: The correct name is Brady Handgun Violence Prevention Act)

13-3109. Sale or gift of firearm to minor; classification

A. Except as provided in subsection C of this section, a person who sells or gives to a minor, without written consent of the minor's parent or legal guardian, a firearm, ammunition or a toy pistol by which dangerous and explosive substances may be discharged is guilty of a class 6 felony.

B. Nothing in this section shall be construed to require reporting sales of firearms, nor shall registration of firearms or firearms sales be required.

C. The temporary transfer of firearms and ammunition by firearms safety instructors, hunter safety instructors, competition coaches or their assistants shall be allowed if the minor's parent or guardian has given consent for the minor to participate in activities such as firearms or hunting safety courses, firearms competition or training. With the consent of the minor's parent or guardian, the temporary transfer of firearms and ammunition by an adult accompanying minors engaged in hunting or formal or informal target shooting activities shall be allowed for those purposes.

13-3111. Minors prohibited from carrying or possessing firearms; exceptions; seizure and forfeiture; penalties

A. Except as provided in subsection B of this section, an unemancipated person who is under eighteen years of age and who is unaccompanied by a parent, grandparent or guardian, or a certified hunter safety instructor or certified firearms safety instructor acting with the consent of the unemancipated person's parent or guardian, shall not knowingly carry or possess on his person, within his immediate control, or in or on a means of transportation a firearm in any place that is open to the public or on any street or highway or on any private property except private property owned or leased by the minor or the minor's parent, grandparent or guardian.

B. This section does not apply to a person who is fourteen, fifteen, sixteen or seventeen years of age and is any of the following:

1. Engaged in lawful hunting or shooting events or marksmanship practice at established ranges or other areas where the discharge of a firearm is not prohibited.

2. Engaged in lawful transportation of an unloaded firearm for the purpose of lawful hunting.

3. Engaged in lawful transportation of an unloaded firearm between the hours of 5:00 a.m. and 10:00 p.m. for the purpose of shooting events or marksmanship practice at established ranges or other areas where the discharge of a firearm is not prohibited.

C. If the minor is not exempt under subsection B of this section and is in possession of a firearm, a peace officer shall seize the firearm at the time the violation occurs.

D. A person who violates subsection A of this section is a delinquent child and shall be subject to the following penalties:

1. For an offense involving an unloaded firearm, a fine of not more than two hundred fifty dollars, and the court may order the suspension or revocation of the person's driver's license until the person reaches eighteen years of age. If the person does not have a driver's license at the time of the adjudication, the court may direct that the department of transportation not issue a driver's license to the person until the person reaches eighteen years of age.

2. For an offense involving a loaded firearm, a fine of not more than five hundred dollars, and the court may order the suspension or revocation of the person's driver's license until the person reaches

eighteen years of age. If the person does not have a driver's license at the time of the adjudication, the court may direct that the department of transportation not issue a driver's license to the person until the person reaches eighteen years of age.

3. For an offense involving a loaded or unloaded firearm, if the person possessed the firearm while the person was the driver or an occupant of a motor vehicle, a fine of not more than five hundred dollars and the court shall order the suspension or revocation of the person's driver's license until the person reaches eighteen years of age. If the person does not have a driver's license at the time of adjudication, the court shall direct that the department of transportation not issue a driver's license to the person until the person reaches eighteen years of age. If the court finds that no other means of transportation is available, the driving privileges of the child may be restricted to travel between the child's home, school and place of employment during specified periods of time according to the child's school and employment schedule.

E. A violation of this section shall be charged, heard and disposed of pursuant to §8-232.

F. Firearms seized pursuant to subsection C of this section shall be held by the law enforcement agency responsible for the seizure until the charges have been adjudicated or disposed of otherwise. Upon adjudication of a person for a violation of this section, the court shall order the firearm forfeited. However, the law enforcement agency shall return the firearm to the lawful owner if the identity of that person is known.

G. If the court finds that the parent or guardian of a minor found responsible for violating this section knew or reasonably should have known of the minor's unlawful conduct and made no effort to prohibit it, the parent or guardian is jointly and severally responsible for any fine imposed pursuant to this section or for any civil actual damages resulting from the unlawful use of the firearm by the minor.

H. This section is supplemental to any other law imposing a criminal penalty for the use or exhibition of a deadly weapon. A minor who violates this section may be prosecuted and convicted for any other criminal conduct involving the use or exhibition of the deadly weapon.

I. This section applies only in counties with populations of more than five hundred thousand persons according to the most recent decennial census. Counties with populations of five hundred thousand persons or less according to the most recent decennial census, or cities or towns within those counties, may adopt an ordinance identical to this section.

(NOTE: Due to clerical error, the following two new laws received the same section number, 13-3112, in the 1994 legislative session.)

13-3112. Permit to carry concealed weapon; violation; classification; qualification; application training program; program instructors; report *(as appears in HB2131)*

A. The department of public safety shall issue a permit to carry a concealed weapon to a person who is qualified under this section. The person shall carry the permit at all times when the person is in actual possession of the concealed weapon and shall present the permit for inspection to any law enforcement officer on request.

B. A permittee who fails to carry the permit at all times that the person is in actual possession of a concealed weapon may have the permit suspended. The department shall be notified of all violations of this section and shall immediately suspend the permit. The permittee shall present the permit to the law enforcement agency or the court. On notification of the presentation of the permit, the department shall restore the permit.

C. A permittee who is arrested or indicted for an offense that would make the person unqualified under the provisions of §13-3101, paragraph 6 or this section shall be immediately suspended and the permit seized. A permittee who becomes unqualified on conviction of such offense shall have the permit revoked. A permittee who is adjudicated not guilty or if the charges are dismissed, shall have the permit restored on presentation of documentation from the court. A permittee who has the charges dropped or dismissed shall have the permit restored on presentation of documentation from the county attorney.

D. A person who fails to present a permit for inspection on the request of a law enforcement officer is guilty of a class 2 misdemeanor.

E. The department of public safety shall issue a permit to an applicant who meets all of the following conditions:

1. Is a resident of this state.

2. Is twenty-one years of age or older.

3. Is not under indictment for and has not been convicted in any jurisdiction of a felony.

4. Does not suffer from mental illness and has not been adjudicated mentally incompetent or committed to a mental institution.

5. Is not unlawfully present in the United States.

6. Satisfactorily completes a firearms safety training program approved by the department of public safety pursuant to subsection N of this section. This paragraph does not apply to a person who has honorably retired as a federal, state or local peace officer with a minimum of ten years of service.

F. The application shall be completed on a form prescribed by the department of public safety. The form shall not require the applicant to disclose the type of firearm for which a permit is sought. The applicant shall attest under penalty of perjury that all of the statements made by the applicant are true. The applicant shall submit the application to the department with a certificate of completion from an approved firearms safety training program, two sets of fingerprints and a reasonable fee determined by the director of the department.

G. On receipt of an application, the department of public safety shall conduct a check of the applicant's criminal history record pursuant to §41-1750. The department of public safety may exchange fingerprint card information with the federal bureau of investigations *(sic)* for national criminal history records checks.

H. The department of public safety shall complete all of the required qualification checks within sixty days after receipt of the application and shall issue a permit within fifteen working days after completing the qualification checks if the applicant meets all of the conditions specified in subsection E of this section. If a permit is denied, the department of public safety shall notify the applicant in writing within fifteen working days after the completion of all of the required qualification checks and shall state the reasons why the application was denied. On receipt of the notification of the denial, the applicant has twenty days to submit any additional documentation to the department. On receipt of the additional documentation, the department shall reconsider its decision and inform the applicant within twenty days of the result of the reconsideration. If denied, the applicant shall be informed of the right to appeal to the superior court.

I. On issuance, a permit is valid for a period of not more four years.

J. The department of public safety shall maintain a computerized permit record system that is accessible to criminal justice agencies for the purpose of confirming the permit status of any person who claims to hold a valid permit. This information shall not be available to any other person or entity except upon order from a state or federal court.

K. A permit issued pursuant to this section is renewable every four years. Before a permit may be renewed, a criminal history record check shall be conducted pursuant to §41-1750, subsection G within sixty days after receipt of the application for renewal.

L. Applications for renewal shall be accompanied by a fee determined by the director of the department of public safety. A certificate of completion of a four-hour refresher firearms safety training program approved by the director of the department is required before a renewal permit may be issued and shall accompany an application for renewal.

M. The department of public safety shall suspend or revoke a permit issued under this section if the permit holder becomes ineligible pursuant to subsection E of this section. The department of public safety shall notify the permit holder in writing within fifteen working days after the revocation or suspension and shall state the reasons for the revocation or suspension.

N. An organization shall apply to the department of public safety for approval of its firearms safety training program. The department shall approve a program that meets the following requirements:

1. Is at least sixteen hours in length.

2. Is conducted on a pass or fail basis.

3. Addresses all of the following topics in a format approved by the director of the department:

(a) Legal issues relating to the use of deadly force.

(b) Weapon care and maintenance.

(c) Mental conditioning for the use of deadly force.

(d) Safe handling and storage of weapons.

(e) Marksmanship.

(f) Judgmental shooting.

4. Is conducted by instructors who submit to a background investigation, including a check for warrants and a criminal history record check.

O. If approved pursuant to subsection N of this section, the organization shall submit two sets of fingerprints from each instructor and a fee to the department pursuant to §41-1750. The department of public safety may exchange this fingerprint card information with the federal bureau of investigations *(sic)* for national criminal history records checks.

P. The proprietary interest of all approved instructors and programs shall be safeguarded and the contents of any training program shall not be disclosed to any person or entity other than a bona fide criminal justice agency, except upon an order from a state or federal court.

Q. If the department of public safety rejects a program, the rejected organization may appeal the decision to the director of the department. On an appeal, the director of the department shall designate another person or persons other than the original reviewer to conduct a hearing. The decision of the hearing officer or officers hearing the appeal is final on the concurrence and signature of the director. The department shall mail written notice of the decision of the hearing officer or officers to the appellant within five working days after the decision. The notice is considered served on mailing.

R. The department of public safety shall maintain information comparing the number of permits requested, the number of permits issued and the number of permits denied. The department shall annually report this information to the governor and the legislature.

S. The director of the department of public safety shall adopt rules for the purpose of implementing and administering the concealed weapons permit program.

13-3112. Adjudicated delinquents; firearm possession; violation; classification
(as appears in SB1356)

A person who was previously adjudicated delinquent and who possesses, uses or carries a firearm within ten years from the date of his adjudication or his release or escape from custody is guilty of a class 5 felony for a first offense and a class 4 felony for a second or subsequent offense if the person was previously adjudicated for an offense that if committed as an adult would constitute:

1. Burglary in the first degree.

2. Burglary in the second degree.

3. Arson.

4. Any felony offense involving the use or threatening exhibition of a deadly weapon or dangerous instrument.

5. An *(sic)* serious offense as defined in §13-604.

CHAPTER 37 • MISCELLANEOUS OFFENSES

13-3708. Introducing a drug, liquor, firearm, weapon or explosive into a juvenile correctional institution; classification

A. A person not authorized by law commits introducing a drug, liquor, firearm, weapon or explosive into a juvenile correctional institution if such person knowingly brings into a state institution for juveniles or within the grounds belonging or adjacent to such institution, any dangerous drug as defined in title 32 or any narcotic drug as defined in title 36, or intoxicating liquor of any kind, or firearms, weapons or explosives of any kind.

B. Introducing a drug, liquor, firearm, weapon or explosive into a juvenile correctional institution is a class 5 felony.

CHAPTER 38 • MISCELLANEOUS

13-3801. Preventing offenses; aiding officer

A. Public offenses may be prevented by intervention of peace officers as follows:

1. By requiring security to keep the peace.

2. Forming a police detail in cities and towns and requiring their attendance in exposed places.

3. Suppressing riots.

B. When peace officers are authorized to act in preventing public offenses, other persons, who, by their command, act in their aid, are justified in so doing.

13-3802. Right to command aid for execution of process; punishment for resisting process

A. When a sheriff or other public officer authorized to execute process finds, or has reason to believe that resistance will be made to execution of the process, such officer may command as many inhabitants of the county as the officer deems proper to assist in overcoming such resistance.

B. The officer shall certify to the court from which the process issued the names of those persons resisting, and they may be proceeded against for contempt of court.

13-3803. Preserving peace at public meetings

The mayor or other officer having direction of the police of a city or town shall order a force, sufficient to preserve the peace, to attend any public meeting when apprehensive of a breach of the peace.

13-3804. Duty of officers to disperse unlawful assembly

A. Where any number of persons, whether armed or not, are unlawfully or riotously assembled, the sheriff and his deputies, officials governing the city or town, or justice of the peace and constables, or any of them, shall go among the persons assembled, or as near to them as possible, and command them, in the name of the state, immediately to disperse.

B. If the people assembled do not immediately disperse, the magistrate and officers shall arrest them, and for that purpose may command the aid of all persons present or within the county.

13-3806. Duty of physician or attendant upon treating certain wounds; classification

A. A physician, surgeon, nurse or hospital attendant called upon to treat any person for gunshot wounds, knife wounds or other material injury which may have resulted from a fight, brawl, robbery or other illegal or unlawful act, shall immediately notify the chief of police or the city marshal, if in an incorporated city or town, or the sheriff, or the nearest police officer, of the circumstances, together with the name and description of the patient, the character of the wound and other facts which may be of assistance to the police authorities in the event the condition of the patient may be due to any illegal transaction or circumstances.

B. Any violation of the provisions of this section by a physician, surgeon, nurse or hospital attendant, is a class 3 misdemeanor.

13-3884. Arrest by private person

A private person may make an arrest:

1. When the person to be arrested has in his presence committed a misdemeanor amounting to a breach of the peace, or a felony.

2. When a felony has been in fact committed and he has reasonable ground to believe that the person to be arrested has committed it.

13-3889. Method of arrest by private person

A private person when making an arrest shall inform the person to be arrested of the intention to arrest him and the cause of the arrest, unless he is then engaged in the commission of an offense, or is pursued immediately after its commission or after an escape, or flees or forcibly resists before the person making the arrest has opportunity so to inform him, or when the giving of such information will imperil the arrest.

13-3892. Right of private person to break into building
A private person, in order to make an arrest where a felony was committed in his presence, as authorized in §13-3884, may break open a door or window of any building in which the person to be arrested is or is reasonably believed to be, if he is refused admittance after he has announced his purpose.

13-3893. Right to break door or window to effect release
When an officer or private person has entered a building in accordance with the provisions of §13-3891 or 13-3892, he may break open a door or window of the building, if detained therein, when necessary for the purpose of liberating himself.

13-3894. Right to break into building in order to effect release of person making arrest detained therein
A peace officer or a private person may break open a door or window of any building when necessary for the purpose of liberating a person who entered the building in accordance with the provisions of §13-3891 or 13-3892 and is detained therein.

13-3895. Weapons to be taken from person arrested
Any person making a lawful arrest may take from the person arrested all weapons which he may have about his person and shall deliver them to the magistrate before whom he is taken.

13-3900. Duty of private person after making arrest
A private person who has made an arrest shall without unnecessary delay take the person arrested before the nearest or most accessible magistrate in the county in which the arrest was made, or deliver him to a peace officer, who shall without unnecessary delay take him before such magistrate. The private person or officer so taking the person arrested before the magistrate shall make before the magistrate a complaint, which shall set forth the facts showing the offense for which the person was arrested. If, however, the officer cannot make the complaint, the private person who delivered the person arrested to the officer shall accompany the officer before the magistrate and shall make to the magistrate the complaint against the person arrested.

13-4305. Seizure of property
A. Property subject to forfeiture under this chapter may be seized for forfeiture by a peace officer:
1. On process issued pursuant to the rules of civil procedure or the provisions of this title including a seizure warrant.
2. By making a seizure for forfeiture on property seized on process issued pursuant to law, including sections 13-3911 through 13-3915.
3. By making a seizure for forfeiture without court process if any of the following is true:
(a) The seizure for forfeiture is of property seized incident to an arrest or search.
(b) The property subject to seizure for forfeiture has been the subject of a prior judgment in favor of this state or any other state or the federal government in a forfeiture proceeding.
(c) The peace officer has probable cause to believe that the property is subject to forfeiture.
B. In determining probable cause for seizure and for forfeiture, the fact that money or any negotiable instrument was found in proximity to contraband or to instrumentalities of an offense gives rise to an inference that the money or instrument was the proceeds of contraband or was used or intended to be used to facilitate commission of the offense.

SOME SIGNIFICANT LAWS FROM OTHER A.R.S. TITLES

Title 4:   Alcoholic Beverages

4-244. Unlawful acts
It is unlawful:

30. For any person other than a peace officer or the licensee or an employee of the licensee acting with the permission of the licensee to be in possession of a firearm while on the licensed premises of an on-sale retail establishment knowing such possession is prohibited. This paragraph shall not be construed to include a situation in which a person is on licensed premises for a limited time in order to seek emergency aid and such person does not buy, receive, consume, or possess spirituous liquor. This paragraph shall not apply to hotel or motel guest room accommodations nor to the exhibit or display of a firearm in conjunction with a meeting, show, class or similar event.

31. For a licensee or employee to knowingly permit a person in possession of a firearm other than a peace officer or the licensee or an employee of the licensee acting with the permission of the licensee to remain on the licensed premises or to serve, sell, or furnish spirituous liquor to a person in possession of a firearm while on the licensed premises of an on-sale retail establishment. This paragraph shall not apply to hotel or motel guest room accommodations nor to the exhibition or display of a firearm in conjunction with a meeting, show, class or similar event. It shall be a defense to action under this paragraph if the licensee or employee requested assistance of a peace officer to remove such person.

4-246. Violation; classification
A. A person violating any provision of this title is guilty of a class 2 misdemeanor unless another classification is prescribed.

Title 12:   Courts and Civil Proceedings

12-820.02. Qualified immunity
Unless a public employee acting within the scope of his employment intended to cause injury or was grossly negligent, neither a public employee nor a public entity is liable for:

1. The failure to make an arrest or the failure to retain an arrested person in custody.

2. An injury caused by an escaping or escaped prisoner or a youth committed to the department of youth treatment and rehabilitation.

3. An injury resulting from the probation, community supervision or discharge of a prisoner or a youth committed to the department of youth treatment and rehabilitation or from the terms and conditions of the prisoner's or youth's probation, community supervision, or from the revocation of the prisoner's or youth's probation, community supervision or conditional release under the psychiatric security review board.

4. An injury caused by a prisoner to any other prisoner or an injury caused by a youth committed to the department of youth treatment and rehabilitation to any other committed youth.

5. The issuance of or failure to revoke or suspend any permit, license, certificate, approval, or similar authorization for which absolute immunity is not provided pursuant to §12-820.01.

6. The failure to discover violations of any provision of law requiring inspections of property other than property owned by the public entity in question.

7. An injury to the driver of a motor vehicle that is attributable to the violation by the driver of §28-692 or 28-693.

8. The failure to prevent the sale or transfer of a handgun to a person whose receipt or possession of the handgun is unlawful under any federal law or any law of this state.

9. Preventing the sale or transfer of a handgun to a person who may lawfully receive or possess a handgun.

Title 15:   Education

15-507.01. Duty to report violations occurring on school premises
All school personnel who observe a violation of §13-3102, subsection A, paragraph 12 or §13-3111 on school premises shall immediately report the violation to the school administrator. The administrator shall immediately report the violation to a peace officer. The peace officer shall report this violation to the department of public safety for inclusion in the statewide and federal uniform crime reports prescribed in §41-1750, subsection A, paragraph 2.

NOTES

NOTES

About the Author

Alan Korwin is a professional writer and management consultant with two decades of experience in business, technical, news and promotional communication. He is a founder and past president of the Arizona Book Publishing Association, on the national publicity committee of the Society for Technical Communication, and a former board member of the Society of Professional Journalists, Valley of the Sun Chapter.

Mr. Korwin helped forge the largest enclave of technologists in the state, as steering committee chair for the Arizona Coalition for Computer Technologies; he did the publicity for Pulitzer Prize cartoonist Steve Benson's 4th book; he wrote a business plan which raised $5 million in venture capital and launched SkyMall; in an executive-level strategic plan he helped American Express define its worldwide telecommunications strategy for the 1990s; and he had a hand in developing ASPED, Arizona's economic strategic plan.

His next book is a co-authored full-color work entitled *Scottsdale, The City and The People*, due out in the fall of 1994. His most recent book is *Wickenburg! The ultimate guide to the ultimate western town*, which features a foreword by Barry Goldwater. Korwin's writing appears regularly in local and national publications.

In 1990 Mr. Korwin introduced a unique seminar entitled, *Instant Expertise—How To Find Out Practically Anything, Fast.* The 4-hour course reveals the trade secrets he uses to gather any information short of espionage. He also teaches writing (How To Get Yourself Published At Last), publishing (The Secret of Self-Publishing), phone power (How to Supercharge Your Telephones) and publicity (The Secret of Free Publicity), at colleges, for businesses and privately. His talk on Constitutional issues (The Pen and The Sword, Constitutional Rights Under Attack) is a real eye opener.

Alan Korwin is originally from New York City, where his clients included IBM, AT&T, NYNEX and others, many with real names. In 1986, finally married, he moved to the Valley of the Sun. It was a joyful and successful move.